COSTING

COSTING
An introduction

STUDENT'S MANUAL

FOURTH EDITION

Colin Drury

Professor, Department of Accountancy and Finance,
University of Huddersfield
UK

INTERNATIONAL THOMSON BUSINESS PRESS
I ⓣ P® An International Thomson Publishing Company

London • Bonn • Johannesburg • Madrid • Melbourne • Mexico City • New York • Paris
Singapore • Tokyo • Toronto • Albany, NY • Belmont, CA • Cincinnati, OH • Detroit, MI

Costing: An Introduction (Student's Manual)

Copyright © 1987, 1990, 1994 and 1999 Colin Drury

 I$\textcircled{T}$P®   A division of International Thomson Publishing Inc.
The ITP log is a trademark under licence

British Library Cataloguing-in-Publication Data
A catalogue record for this book is available from the British Library

First edition 1987
Second edition 1990, reprinted 1993
Third edition 1994, reprinted 1995 (all published by Chapman & Hall)
Third edition reprinted 1996 by International Thomson Business Press

Fourth edition 1999 by International Thomson Business Press

Typeset by Columns, Reading, Berkshire
Printed in the UK by The Alden Press, Osney Mead, Oxford

ISBN 1-86152-275-4

International Thomson Business Press
Berkshire House
168–173 High Holborn
London WC1V 7AA
UK

http://www.itbp.com

Contents

Preface   vii

2   Cost and revenue classification
    Answers to Chapter 2   1
3   Accounting for materials and labour
    Answers to Chapter 3   11
4   Accounting for overhead expenditure
    Answers to Chapter 4   23
5   Accounting entries for a job costing system
    Answers to Chapter 5   39
6   Process costing
    Answers to Chapter 6   57
7   Joint product and by-product costing
    Answers to Chapter 7   71
8   Absorption costing and variable costing
    Answers to Chapter 8   81
9   Cost–volume–profit analysis
    Answers to Chapter 9   91
10   Measuring costs and benefits for decision-making
    Answers to Chapter 10   111
11   Activity-based costing
    Answers to Chapter 11   127
12   Capital investment decisions
    Answers to Chapter 12   131
13   The budgeting process
    Answers to Chapter 13   139
14   Control in the organization
    Answers to Chapter 14   155
15   Standard costing and variance analysis
    Answers to Chapter 15   167
16   Planning and control of stock levels
    Answers to Chapter 16   193

Preface

This manual is complementary to the main textbook *Costing: An introduction.* Throughout the main book I have kept the illustrations simple to enable the reader to understand the principles involved in designing and evaluating management and cost accounting systems. More complex problems are provided at the end of each chapter so that the student can pursue certain topics in more depth, and concentrate on the application of principles. The objective of this manual is to provide solutions to the problems which have an asterisk beside the question number and, where necessary, to supplement the main text with a discussion of the additional issues raised by the questions.

The solutions given in this manual are my own and not the approved solution of the professional body setting the problem. Where an essay question is asked and a full answer requires undue repetition of the book, either references are made to the appropriate sections of the main book, or an answer guide or outline is provided. You should note that there will be no 'ideal' answer to problems which are not strictly numerical. Answers are provided which, it is felt, would be generally acceptable in most contexts. Where possible the problems are arranged in ascending order of difficulty. A short description of each problem is given at the beginning of each chapter of this manual.

Finally I would like to thank, once again, the Institute of Chartered Accountants in England and Wales, the Chartered Association of Certified Accountants, the Chartered Institute of Cost and Management Accountants, the Association of Accounting Technicians, the Joint Matriculation Board and the Associated Examining board for permission to reproduce problems which have appeared in past examinations.

Cost and revenue classification

Answers to Chapter 2

Question summary

2.1 to 2.5
Multiple choice questions.

2.6 to 2.12
Essay questions on cost classification. Note that Question 2.9 also includes a discussion of the role of the cost accountant. The answers to some of these questions are contained within the chapter and therefore the answers consist of a reference to the appropriate section in Chapter 2.

2.13
A multiple choice style question relating to cost behaviour.

2.14
An essay question requiring a description of different cost terms.

2.15 to 2.17
Short questions which can be used to test your understanding of cost classification.

2.18
A description of various cost terms – discretionary, variable, fixed, notional and opportunity costs. The question also requires the student to indicate whether a project should be continued or abandoned based on a comparison of relevant revenues with relevant costs.

2.19
A more demanding and time-consuming Foundation/Stage 1 question relating to cost behaviour.

2.20
Calculation of a product cost and extraction of relevant costs for decision-making.

2.21
Calculation of a product costs for cost-plus pricing.

2.22
Computation and discussion of relevant, sunk and opportunity costs for decision-making.

2.23
Ascertaining the relevant cost of car journeys and the estimation of costs at 80% of budgeted activity.

Answer to question 2.1

Item (B) will be constant within the relevant range of output.
Item (C) will be constant per unit.
If output declines fixed cost per *unit* will decrease.
Total variable cost will fall in line with a decline in output and therefore item A is the correct answer.

Answer to question 2.2

Total variable overheads = 17,000 × £3.50 = £59,500.
Total variable overhead (£59,500) + Total fixed overhead = Total overhead (£246,500).
Total fixed overhead = £246,500 − £59,500 = £187,000.
Answer = C

Answer to question 2.3

Answer = B

Answer to question 2.4

Answer = B

Answer to question 2.5

Answer = B

Answer to question 2.6

See the description of cost behaviour in the sections in Chapter 2 on classification of costs for decision-making and classification of costs for control for the answer to these questions. In particular the answer should provide graphs for fixed costs, variable costs, semi-fixed costs and semi-variable costs.

Answer to question 2.7

You will find the answer to this question in Chapter 2. In particular the answer should describe the classification of costs for stock valuation and profit measurement; classification for decision-making and planning; classification for control. In addition the answer should illustrate methods of classification (see Chapter 2 for examples) within the above categories and describe the benefits arising from classifying costs in the manner illustrated.

Answer to question 2.8

See Chapter 2 for the answer to this question.

Answer to question 2.9

(a) See the section on the role of the management accountant in the management process in Chapter 1 for the answer to this question. In particular your answer should stress that the cost accountant provides financial information for stock valuation purposes and also presents relevant information to management for decision-making and planning and cost control purposes. For example, the cost accountant provides information on the costs and revenues of alternative courses of action to assist management in selecting the course of action which will maximize future cash flows. By coordinating plans together in the form of budgets and comparing actual performance with plans the accountant can pinpoint those activities which are not proceeding according to plan.

(b) (i) Direct costs are those costs which can be traced to a cost objective. If the cost objective is a sales territory then *fixed* salaries of salesmen will be a direct cost. Therefore the statement is incorrect.

(ii) Whether a cost is controllable depends on the level of authority and time span being considered. For example. a departmental foreman may have no control over the number of supervisors employed in his department but this decision may be made by his superior. In the long term such costs are controllable.

(iii) This statement is correct. See the section on sunk costs in Chapter 2 for an explanation of why this statement is correct.

Answer to question 2.10

See Chapter 2 for the answer to this question.

Answer to question 2.11

Cost information is required for the following purposes:

(a)   costs for stock valuation and profit measurement;
(b)   costs for decision-making;
(c)   costs for planning and control.

For the alternative measures of cost that might be appropriate for each of the above purposes see Chapter 2.

Answer to question 2.12

(i)   See Chapter 2 for a definition of opportunity cost and sunk cost.
(ii)   *Opportunity cost*: If scarce resources such as machine hours are required for a special contract then the cost of the contract should include the lost profit that would have been earned on the next best alternative. This should be recovered in the contract price.
Sunk cost: The original cost of equipment used for a contract is a sunk cost and should be ignored. The change in the resale value resulting from the use of the equipment represents the relevant cost of using the equipment.
(iii)   The significance of opportunity cost is that relevant costs do not consist only of future cash outflows associated directly with a particular course of action. Imputed costs must also be included.
    The significance of sunk costs is that past costs are not relevant for decision-making.

Answer to question 2.13

Total fixed costs will remain unchanged in the short term (within the relevant range) and variable costs are constant per unit. If output declines fixed costs per unit will increase. The correct answer is Option A, since total variable costs should decline if output is less than the original budget.

Answer to question 2.14

See Chapter 2 for an explanation of the terms avoidable costs, unavoidable costs and cost centres. A cost unit is a unit of product or service for which costs are ascertained. In a manufacturing organization a cost unit will be a unit of output produced within a cost centre. In a service organization, such as an educational establishment, a cost unit might be the cost per student.

Answer to question 2.15

(a) Production overhead: 1, 3, 8, 9, 14, 16.
Selling and distribution overhead: 2, 5, 7, 10, 11.
Administration overhead: 6, 13, 15.
Research and development overhead: 4, 12.

(b) Direct labour might be regarded as a fixed cost rather than a variable cost for the following reasons:
   (i) Legislation may prevent dismissal of employees or redundancy costs may be too excessive to justify dismissal when a firm encounters temporary slack periods.
   (ii) Production workers tend to be paid fixed salaries irrespective of the level of output.
   (iii) Workers are no longer dismissed during slack periods.

Answer to question 2.18

(a) A large proportion of non-manufacturing costs are of a discretionary nature. In respect of such costs. management has some significant range of discretion as to the amount it will budget for the particular activity in question. Examples of discretionary costs (sometimes called *managed* or *programmed costs*) include advertising, research and development, and training costs. There is no optimum relationship between inputs (as measured by the costs) and outputs (as measured by revenues or some other objective function) for these costs. Furthermore, they are not predetermined by some previous commitment. In effect, management can determine what quantity of service it wishes to purchase. For example, it can choose to spend small or large amounts on research and development or advertising. The great difficulty in controlling such costs is that there is no established method for determining the appropriate amount to be spent in particular periods.

   For a description of fixed and variable costs see Chapter 2. Examples of fixed costs include depreciation of the factory building, supervisors' salaries and charges. Examples of variable costs include direct materials, power and sales commissions.

(b) The £500,000 is a sunk cost and cannot be avoided. It is therefore not a relevant cost for decision-making purposes. The project should be continued because the incremented/relevant benefits exceed the incremental/relevant costs:

	£000
Incremental benefits	350
Incremental costs	200
Net incremental benefit	150

(c) An opportunity cost is a cost that measures the opportunity lost or sacrificed when the choice of one course of action requires that an alternative course of action be given up. The following are examples of opportunity costs:

(i) If scarce resources such as machine hours are required for a special contract then the opportunity cost represents the lost profit that would have been earned from the alternative use of the machine hours.

(ii) If an employee is paid £5 per hour and is charged out at £11 per hour for committed work then, if that employee is redirected to other work, the lost contribution of £6 per hour represents the opportunity cost of the employee's time.

The CIMA terminology defines a notional cost as: 'A hypothetical cost taken into account in a particular situation to represent a benefit enjoyed by an entity in respect of which no actual cost is incurred.' The following are examples of notional costs:

(i) interest on capital to represent the notional cost of using an asset rather than investing the capital elsewhere;

(ii) including rent as a cost for premises owned by the company so as to represent the lost rent income resulting from using the premises for business purposes.

Answer to question 2.19

(a) (i) *Schedule of annual mileage costs:*

	5,000 miles £	10,000 miles £	15,000 miles £	30,000 miles £
Variable costs:				
Spares	100	200	300	600
Petrol	380	760	1,140	2,280
Total variable cost	480	960	1,440	2,880
Variable cost per mile	0.096	0.096	0.096	0.096
Fixed costs				
Depreciation[a]	2,000	2,000	2,000	2,000
Maintenance	120	120	120	120
Vehicle licence	80	80	80	80
Insurance	150	150	150	150
Tyres[b]	–	–	75	150
	2,350	2,350	2,425	2,500
Fixed cost per mile	0.47	0.235	0.162	0.083
Total cost	2,830	3,310	3,865	5,380
Total cost per mile	0.566	0.331	0.258	0.179

Notes:

[a] Annual depreciation $= \dfrac{£5,500 \text{ (cost)} - £1,500 \text{ (trade-in price)}}{2 \text{ years}} = £2,000$

[b] At 15,000 miles per annum tyres will be replaced once during the two-year period at a cost of £150.

The average cost per year is £75. At 30,000 miles per annum tyres will be replaced once each year.

Comments:

Tyres are a semi-fixed cost. In the above calculations they have been regarded as a step fixed cost. An alternative approach would be to regard the semi-fixed cost as a variable cost by dividing £150 tyre replacement by 25,000 miles. This results in a variable cost per mile of £0.006. For a discussion of the alternative treatment of semi-fixed costs see Chapter 2.

Depreciation and maintenance cost have been classified as fixed costs. They are likely to be semi-variable costs, but in the absence of any additional information they have been classified as fixed costs.

(ii)   See Figure Q2.19.

(iii) The respective costs can be obtained from the vertical dashed lines in the graph (Figure Q2.19).

(b)   The *cost per mile* declines as activity increases. This is because the majority of costs are fixed and do not increase when mileage increases. However, total cost will increase with increases in mileage.

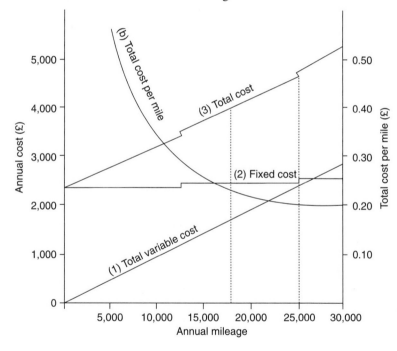

Figure Q2.19 *The step increase in fixed cost is assumed to occur at an annual mileage of 12,500 miles and 25,000 miles, because tyres are assumed to be replaced at this mileage.*

Answer to question 2.22

(a)   (i)   For an explanation of sunk and opportunity costs see Chapter 2. The down payment of £5,000 represents a sunk cost. The lost profit from subletting the shop of £1,600 p.a. ((£550 × 12) − £5,000) is an example of an opportunity cost. Note that only the £5,000 additional rental is included in the opportunity cost calculation. (The £5,000 sunk cost is excluded from the calculation.)

(ii) The relevant information for running the shop is:

	£
Net sales	100,000
Costs (£87,000 − £5,000 sunk cost)	82,000
	18,000
Less opportunity cost from subletting	1,600
Profit	16,400

The above indicates that £16,400 additional profits will be obtained from using the shop for the sale of clothing. It is assumed that Mrs Johnson will not suffer any other loss of income if she devotes half her time to running the shop.

(b) The CIMA terminology defines a notional cost as 'A hypothetical cost taken into account in a particular situation to represent a benefit enjoyed by an entity in respect of which no actual expense is incurred.' Examples of notional cost include:

(i) Interest on capital to represent the notional cost of using an asset rather than investing the capital elsewhere.

(ii) Including rent as a cost for premises owned by the company so as to represent the lost rent income resulting from using the premises for business purposes.

Answer to question 2.23

(a) See Chapter 2 for a description of opportunity costs. Out of pocket cost can be viewed as being equivalent to incremental or relevant costs as described in Chapter 2.

(b) Depreciation is not a relevant cost since it will be the same for both alternatives. It is assumed that tyres and miscellaneous represent the additional costs incurred in travelling to work. The relevant costs are:

Using the car to travel to work:

	£
Petrol	128
Tyres and miscellaneous	52
	180
Contribution from passenger	120
Relevant cost	60

Using the train:

Relevant cost	£188

(c)	£000	£000	%
Sales		2,560.0	100
Direct materials	819.2		32
Direct wages	460.8		18
Variable production overhead	153.6		6
Variable administration/selling	76.8		3
Total variable cost		1,510.4	59
Contribution		1,049.6	41
Fixed production overhead[a]	768		30
Fixed administration/selling[b]	224		8.75
		992	
Profit		57.6	2.25

Notes:
[a] $100/80 \times £2,560,000 \times 0.24$
[b] $100/80 \times £2,560,000 \times 0.07$

Accounting for materials and labour

Answers to Chapter 3

Question summary

3.1
Multiple choice question.

3.2 to 3.8
Various essay questions on topics related to Chapter 3.

3.9 to 3.12
Computations for various stores pricing methods. Questions 3.10 and 3.12 also require the calculation of EOQ. In addition, the final part of Question 3.12 requires the computation of maximum and minimum stock levels and the reorder point.

3.13
This question consists of two parts: stores pricing and labour cost accounting.

3.14
A simple question which is useful for illustrating some of the issues to be considered when introducing an incentive scheme.

3.15 to 3.17
Calculation of earnings based on hourly rates, piecework and bonus schemes.

3.18
Accounting treatment of holiday pay and overtime plus a computation and evaluation of a time rate and incentive payment system.

3.19
Calculation of labour turnover percentage and efficiency ratio and a discussion of how labour turnover can be reduced.

3.20 and 3.21
These are more difficult problems which focus on the effects of introducing incentive schemes.

Answer to question 3.1

Answer = D

Answer to question 3.3

Your reply should indicate that there is a need to verify that actual stocks should agree with the computerized records. It is likely that computerized records will be more reliable than a clerical recording system. Nevertheless, errors may still exist. In addition there is the problem of theft and wastage. It is therefore important that physical stocks be checked periodically with the computerized records. Your answer should stress that a continuous system of stocktaking is preferable to the alternative of a complete periodic system of stocktaking.

Answer to question 3.5

(a) With a computer-based system orders for receipts, issues and returns of materials can be input usually with more speed and accuracy than a manual system. Stock issue prices and balances will be automatically determined by the computer program. For each item of stock, control levels, such as minimum and maximum stock levels and the reorder level, can be set up. The computer-based system will automatically highlight those stock items which are outside the control levels and this will minimize stockouts and overstocking. With a computerized system purchase requisitions are automatically generated when stocks reach their reorder point.

(b) The answer should describe goods received notes, stores requisitions and purchase requisitions. See Chapter 3 for a description of these items.

Answer to question 3.6

(a) The managing director's conclusions are incorrect because:
  (i)   Purchases may be in excess of materials used to produce goods for sale. In other words, raw material stocks may have increased.
  (ii) Material prices might have increased but the quantity of materials purchased or used remains unchanged.
  (iii) Stocks of WIP and finished goods may have increased, thus requiring more purchases.
  (iv) The actual selling price may have been lower than expected.

(b) Material losses may have occurred because of the following:
  (i)   Purchase of inferior quality materials resulting in excessive wastage. This might be overcome by setting standards indicating the qualities required. If certain suppliers are known for the higher quality materials a list of such suppliers should be kept. Close cooperation is essential between the production departments and the purchasing department,

and the reporting system should be designed so that the purchasing department is immediately informed when inferior quality materials are purchased so that steps can be taken to avoid this occurring again in the future.

(ii) Use of inefficient and unskilled labour. This might be overcome by improving training.

(iii) Obsolete stocks. This can be reduced by setting maximum, minimum and reorder stock levels and regularly checking on the frequency of issues. A report on obsolete stocks should be prepared for management at frequent intervals, indicating the reasons for the obsolescence. All purchase requisitions should be initiated only by the storekeeper, who should check the stock levels prior to completing the purchase requisition.

Answer to question 3.11

(a) (i) See Chapter 3 for an explanation of continuous stocktaking

(ii) Perpetual inventory is a system of entering details of receipts and issues for each individual item of materials onto a record card. A separate record is maintained for each individual item of material. Therefore the quantity of stock on hand can be ascertained at any point in time. In most organizations stock records are maintained in a computerized format.

(b) (i)

Date	Receipts Quantity	Receipts Price £	Receipts Value £	Issues Quantity	Issues Price £	Issues Value £	Balance Quantity	Balance Price £	Balance Value £
Day 1							3,040	0.765	2,325.60
1	1,400	0.780	1,092				4,440	0.770	3,417.60
2				1,700	0.770	1,309	2,740	0.770	2,108.60
3	60	0.770	46.20				2,800	0.770	2,154.80
4				220	0.780	171.60	2,580	0.769	1,983.20
4	1,630	0.778	1,268.14				4,210	0.772	3,251.34
5				1,250	0.772	965	2,960	0.772	2,286.34

Material X Account

	£		£
Opening stock	2,325.60	Work-in-progress	1,309.00
Cost ledger control	1,092.00	Cost ledger control	171.60
Work-in-progress	46.20	Work-in-progress	965.00
Cost ledger control	1,268.14	Closing stock	2,286.34
	4,731.94		4,731.94

Answer to question 3.12

(a) (i) Two of the following methods of pricing should be selected:

FIFO

Date	Receipts		Issues		Balance	
	kg	£	kg	£	Number	£
1 Nov.					20,000	60,000
3 Nov.	5,000	20,000			25,000	80,000
10 Nov.	12,000	60,000			37,000	140,000
17 Nov.			20,000 at £3 = £60,000			
			4,000 at £4 = £16,000		13,000	64,000
20 Nov.	17,000	76,500			30,000	140,500
27 Nov.			1,000 at £4 = £4,000			
			12,000 at £5 = £60,000			
			7,000 at £4.50 = £31,500		10,000	45,000

LIFO

Date	Receipts		Issues	Balance			
	kg	£		kg	£	Number	£
1 Nov.						20,000	60,000
3 Nov.	5,000	20,000				25,000	80,000
10 Nov.	12,000	60,000				37,000	140,000
17 Nov.				12,000 at £5 = £60.00			
				5,000 at £4 = £20,000			
				7,000 at £3 = £21,000		13,000	39,000
20 Nov.	17,000	76,500				30,000	115,500
27 Nov.				17,000 at £4.50 = £76,500			
				3,000 at £3 = £9,000		10,000	30,000

Averaged weighted cost

Date	Receipts		Issues		Balance	
	kg	£	kg	£	Number	£
1 Nov.					20,000 at £3	= 60,000
3 Nov.	5,000	20,000			25,000 at £3.20	= 80,000
10 Nov.	12,000	60,000			37,000 at £3.78	= 140,000
17 Nov.			24,000 at £3.78 = 90,720		13,000 at £3.78	= 49,280
20 Nov.	17,000	76,500			30,000 at £4.19	= 125,780
27 Nov.			20,000 at £4.19 = 83,800		10,000 at £4.19	= 41,980

(ii) Job 124

	FIFO £	LIFO £	W/Average £
Direct material (Total issues)	171,500	186,500	174,520
Direct labour	50,000	50,000	50,000
Overhead	188,650	205,150	191,972
Total cost	410,150	441,650	416,492
Profit	45,572	49,072	46,400
Selling price	455,722	490,722	462,894

(iii) LIFO has produced a higher material cost and as a consequence a higher selling price to reflect the upward trend in material costs compared to FIFO. However, the valuation of stock under LIFO is a lot lower than FIFO as it is based upon older stock. Weighted average arrives at figures between the extremities of FIFO and LIFO but is not an actual cost. Note the effect on overhead of using direct material as a basis of recovery.

(b) (i) See the sections on complete periodic stockcount and continuous stock-taking in Chapter 3 for an evaluation of continuous stocktaking. The advantages of continuous stocktaking are that:
(1) There is no need to stop production for stocktaking thus saving production costs.
(2) Discrepancies are highlighted earlier than with periodic stocktaking.

(ii) The advantages of centralized stores are as follows:
(1) Economies of scale (e.g. fewer staff and lower stocks).
(2) Better control and security of stocks.
(3) Duplication of stocks can he avoided.
However. if production centres are located a long way from the centralized stores there may be long delays in obtaining materials. It may also be costly in terms of transportation costs.

(c) (i) Economic order quantity

$$= \sqrt{\frac{2DO}{H}}$$

D = Annual demand
O = Cost of ordering/per order
H = Holding cost per item

$$= \sqrt{\frac{2 \times 400 \times 50 \times 150}{2}}$$

= 1,732 kilos

(ii) Reorder level
= Maximum usage × maximum lead time
= 600 × 3 = 1,800 units

(iii) Minimum level of stock
= Reorder level − average usage in average lead time
= 1,800 − (2 × 400) = 1,000 units

(iv) Maximum level of stock that should be held
= Reorder level + EOQ − minimum usage in minimum lead time
= 1,800 + 1,732 − (400 × 1) = 3,132.

Answer to question 3.13

(a) (i) *FIFO*: Because the units contained in the closing stock are less than the most recent purchase quantity, the value of the closing stock will be based on the price per unit of the most recent purchase. Therefore the value of the closing stock is £123.20, consisting of 44 units at £2.80 per unit.

(ii) *LIFO:*

	Receipts	Issues
Opening stock	35 at £2.00	
2.11.81		25 at £2
5.11.81	40 at £2.25	
10.11.81		38 at £2.25
13.11.81	30 at £2.50	
23.11.81	50 at £2.80	
24.11.81		48 at £2.80

From the above schedule we can see that the closing stock consists of the following purchases:

	£
Opening stock (10 at £2)	20.00
5 November purchase (2 at £2.25)	4.50
13 November purchase (30 at £2.50)	75.00
23 November purchase (2 at £2.80)	5.60
Closing stock	105.10

(b) The value of material issued on 24 November is £125.76 and is calculated as follows:

	Receipts			Issues			Closing balance		
	Quantity	Price	Value	Quantity	Price	Value	Quantity	Price	Value
		£	£		£	£		£	£
1.11.81	–	–	–	–	–	–	35	2.00	70.00
2.11.81	–	–	–	25	2.00	50.00	10	2.00	20.00
5.11.81	40	2.25	90	–	–	–	50	2.20	110.00
10.11.81	–	–	–	38	2.20	83.60	12	2.20	26.40
13.11.81	30	2.50	75	–	–	–	42	2.41	101.40
23.11.81	50	2.80	140	–	–	–	92	2.62	241.40
24.11.81	–	–	–	48	2.62	125.76	44	2.62	115.64

The cost of the 10 units issued to replace those previously damaged should be charged (debited) to a scrap account and the stores ledger control account should be reduced (credited). The issue cost represents abnormal scrap, which should not be included in the stock valuation. Therefore cost of the scrap should be written off as a period cost. If the scrap was considered to be a normal unavoidable cost inherent in the production process then it would be reasonable to charge the cost of the normal scrap to the job. For a discussion of the treatment of normal and abnormal losses see Chapter 6.

(c) *Calculation of total hours worked:*

	Hours
Normal hours (£4,800/£3 per hour)	1,600
Overtime hours (£1,440/£4.50 per hour)	320
	1,920

Allocation of wages cost:

	£
Capital expenditure (60 hours at £3)	180
Non-productive time (280 hours at £3)	840
Productive time (balance of £1,580 hours (1,920 − 340 at £3)	4,740
Overtime premium (320 hours at £1.50)	480
Shift premium	360
	6,600

The journal entries are as follows:

	Dr	Cr
Wages control account	6,600	
Cost ledger control account[a]		6,600
Work in progress account	4,740	
Capital equipment account	180	
Production overhead account (840 + 480 + 360)	1,680	
Wages control account		6,600

Note:

[a]For an explanation of this account see the section on interlocking accounting in Chapter 5.

Answer to question 3.15

(a) *Advantages:*
   (i) Both the firm and the employee should benefit from the introduction of an incentive scheme. Employees should receive an increase in wages arising from the increased production. The firm should benefit from a reduction in the fixed overhead per unit and an increase in sales volume.
   (ii) The opportunity to earn higher wages may encourage efficient workers to join the company.
   (iii) Morale may be improved if extra effort is rewarded.
   Disadvantages:
   (i) Incentive schemes can be complex and difficult to administer.
   (ii) Establishing performance levels leads to frequent and continuing disputes.
   (iii) The quality of the output may decline.

(b)

(i) Hourly rate

Employee A $38 \times £3 = £114$

Employee B $36 \times £2 = £72$

Employee C $40 \times £2.50 = £100$

Employee D $34 \times £3.60 = £122.40$

(ii) Piecework

Employee A $(42 \times £0.30) + (72 \times £0.45) + (92 \times £0.75) = £114$

Employee B $(120 \times £0.30) + (76 \times £0.45) = £70.20$

Employee C $(50 \times £0.75) = £37.50$

Employee D $(120 \times £0.30) + (270 \times £0.45) = £157.50$

Note that with the piecework system the employees are paid an agreed rate per unit produced. The piece rates are £0.30 per unit of x (6 minutes × £0.05), £0.45 for y (9 × £0.05) and £0.75 for z (15 × £0.05). Only employee C earns less than 75% of basic pay. Therefore C will receive a gross wage of £75. The piece rate wages should be charged directly to the products and the difference between the guaranteed minimum wage of £75 and the piecework wage of £37.50 for employee C should be charged to an appropriate overhead account.

With a bonus scheme, a set time is allowed for each job and a bonus is paid based on the proportion of time saved. The calculations for each employee are:

Time allowed (hours)		Time saved (hours)	Bonus £	Total wages £
A $(42 \times 6/60) + (72 \times 9/60) + (92 \times 15/60)$	= 38	0	0	114
B $(120 \times 6/60) + (76 \times 9/60)$	= 23.4	0	0	72
C $(50 \times 15/60)$	= 12.5	0	0	100
D $(120 \times 6/60) + (270 \times 9/60)$	= 52.5	18.5	$\frac{2}{3} \times 18.5 \times £3.60$ = £44.40	£122.40 + £44.40

Employees A, B and C do not earn a bonus, because the time taken is in excess of time allowed.

Answer to question 3.17

(a)

(i)

		Y £		Z £	
	Time-based earnings	154	$(44 \times £3.50)$	180	$(40 \times £4.50)$
	Guaranteed minimum (80%)	123.20		144	
	Piecework earnings	168	$(480 \times £0.35)$	136.50	$(390 \times £0.35)$
	Earnings	£168		£144	
(ii)	Time taken	44 hrs		40 hrs	
	Time allowed	56 hrs	$(480 \times 7/60)$	45.5 hrs	$(390 \times 7/60)$
	Time saved	12 hrs		5.5 hrs	
	Bonus hours (75% of time saved)	9 hrs		4.125 hrs	
	Hours paid	53 hrs		44.125 hrs	
	Earnings	£185.50		£198.56	

(b) Time rate bases are preferable when:
   (i)   quality is more important than quantity;
   (ii) employees have little control over their output.

Answer to question 3.18

(a) For the answer to this question you should refer to the sections on elements of manufacturing cost in Chapter 2 and accounting treatment of various labour cost items in Chapter 3.

(b)　*Current system:*

Total weekly wages	£960 (6 × £160)
Weekly wage per employee	£160 (£960/6 employees)
Average output per employee	1,000 units (6,000 units/6)
Labour cost per unit of output	16p (£960/6,000 units)

New system:

Average output per employee	1,000 units (6,600 units/6)
Weekly wage per employee	£180 (800 × 16p) + (200 × 17p) + (100 × 18p)
Total weekly wages	£1,080 (£180 × 6)
Labour cost per unit of output	16.36p (£1,080/6,600 units)

Note that the above calculations are based on the assumption that each individual produces the average output of 1,100 units per week. If this is not the case then total wages will differ slightly from the above figure.

With time-based remuneration systems, workers are paid for the number of hours attended at the basic wage rate. An additional premium over the base rate is paid for overtime. The merits of time-based systems are that they are simple to administer and easy to understand. The weekly wage is known in advance and does not fluctuate with changes in output. Time rate systems have a number of disadvantages. In particular, there is no motivation to increase output, and this can result in a greater need for supervision. Time-based systems are most appropriate where the quality of the output is particularly important or where the workers have little influence over the volume of production.

With individual performance-based remuneration systems, wages paid are related to output. The merits of performance-based systems are that effort and efficiency are rewarded, and this generally results in higher wages, improved morale and the ability to attract efficient workers. In the above illustration, on average, each employee's wage increases by £20 per week (a 12.5% increase). The employer gains from increased production, higher sales revenue and a decrease in unit fixed costs. Labour cost per unit has increased in the above illustration, but it is likely that this will be compensated for by a lower fixed overhead cost per unit and additional sales revenue.

Individual performance-based remuneration systems suffer from the following disadvantages:

(i)　Some workers may suffer a decline in wages. For example, a worker who produces 900 units per week would receive a weekly wage of £145 (800 × 16p plus 100 × 17p), a decline of £15 per week.

(ii)　Performance-based systems are more complex and expensive to administer, and can result in complex negotiations and frequent disputes.

(iii)　Quality of output might suffer.

Answer to question 3.19

(a)　Labour turnover percentage

$$\frac{\text{Number of employees leaving during the period (7)}}{\text{Average total number of employees for the period (42)}} \times 100$$

= 16.7%

(b) Possible reasons for the labour turnover include:
(i) Promotion either within or outside the firm.
(ii) Personal circumstances such as moving from the area, retirement, pregnancy.
(iii) Dissatisfaction with pay or working conditions.
The costs of labour turnover include leaving, recruitment and training costs. Leaving costs include the costs associated with completing the appropriate documentation and lost production if the employees cannot be immediately replaced. Recruitment costs result from the advertising, selection and engagement of new staff. Training costs include costs associated with lost production when training is being given, defective work and low productivity during the training period.
Labour turnover and associated costs can be reduced by ensuring that;
(i) pay and working conditions are satisfactory and comparable with alternative employers;
(ii) adequate training is provided;
(iii) an appropriate career structure exists.

(c) The time allowed for 114,268 units is 5,194 hours (114,268/22)

Efficiency ratio = Time allowed (standard hours)/actual hours
= 5,194 hours/4,900 hours
= 106%

Therefore the labour rate is £4.738 per hour (£4.60 × 103/100)
Standard cost = £23,892 (5,194 hours at £4.60)
Actual cost = £23,216 4,900 hours at £4.738)
Variance = £676 Favourable

Answer to question 3.20

(i) Current average maximum production = 30 × 55 hrs × 6 units = 9,900 units
Proposed maximum production = 30 × 55 hrs × 8 units = 13,200 units

Existing payment system:

Output levels (units)	7,000	9,600	9,900
	£	£	£
Sales value (£10 per unit)	70,000	96,000	99,000
Pre-finishing VC	56,000	76,800	79,200
Direct labour:			
Guaranteed	3,600	3,600	3,600
Overtime (*W1*)	–	1,800	2,025
Variable overhead (*W2*)	560	768	792
Fixed overhead	9,000	9,000	9,000
Total cost	69,160	91,968	94,617
Profit	840	4,032	4,383

Proposed scheme:

Output levels (units)	7,000	9,600	9,900	12,000
	£	£	£	£
Sales value	70,000	96,000	99,000	120,000
Pre-finishing VC	56,000	76,800	79,200	96,000
Direct labour at				
£0.55 per unit	3,850	5,280	5 445	6,600
Variable overhead (*W3*)	420	576	594	720
Fixed overhead	9,000	9,000	9,000	9,000
Total cost	69,270	91,656	94,239	112,320
Profit	730	4,344	4,761	7,680

Working:

(*W1*) 9,600 units requires 1,600 hrs (9,600/6), $\therefore$ Overtime = 400 hrs $\times$ 4.50
9,900 units requires 1,650 hrs (9,900/6), $\therefore$ Overtime = 450 hrs $\times$ £4.50
Basic hours = 1,200 hrs

(*W2*) 7,000 units = 7,000/6 $\times$ £0.48, 9,600 units = 9,600/6 $\times$ £0.48, 9,900 units
= 9,900/6 $\times$ £0.48

(*W3*) 7,000 units = 7,000/8 $\times$ £0.48, 9,600 units = 9,600/8 $\times$ £0.48, 9,900 units
= 9,900/8 $\times$ £0.48
12,000 units = 12,000/8 $\times$ £0.48

(ii) At low output levels the average wage rate per unit is £0.50 (£3/6 hrs), compared with £0.55 with the incentive scheme. However, once overtime is worked, the wage rate per unit of output is £0.75 (£4.50/6), compared with £0.55 per unit under the incentive scheme. Overtime starts at 7,200 units (1,200 hrs $\times$ 6 units). Hence savings will increase with the incentive scheme beyond 7,200 units.

Variable overheads vary with productive hours. Therefore variable overhead per unit will be £0.08 (£0.48/6) under the old scheme and £0.06 per unit under the new scheme (£0.48/8).

The proposed incentive scheme will also enable the maximum output level to be achieved, thus enabling maximum sales demand to be achieved.

Accounting for overhead expenditure

Answers to Chapter 4

4.1 to 4.4
Multiple choice questions.

4.5 to 4.7
Discussion questions relating to Chapter 4.

4.8 to 4.13
Questions which require the apportionment of overheads, the preparation of overhead analysis statements and the calculation of departmental overhead rates. Questions 4.8, 4.10, 4.11 and 4.13 also require the calculation of product costs. Part (d) of Question 4.13 requires the preparation of an overhead control account. This topic is dealt with in Chapter 5.

4.14
Job cost calculation.

4.15 to 4.22
Calculation and discussion of different overhead absorption rates. Questions 4.16 to 4.19 also require the calculation of under-/over-recovery of overheads. In addition, Question 4.18 requires an analysis of the under-/over-recovery of overheads and a discussion of predetermined versus actual overhead rates. Question 4.20 involves the reallocation of service department overheads and 4.21 requires the separation of fixed and variable overheads using the high-low method.

4.23
Calculation of overhead absorption rates and product costs and a make-or-buy decision.

4.24 to 4.27
Reapportionment of service department costs. Question 4.25 also requires a product cost calculation and the selection of the most suitable overhead recovery method.

4.28
Requires the calculation of overhead absorption rates and extraction of variable costs for a make-or-buy decision. This question is useful for emphasizing the decision-making aspects at this stage. Alternatively. you may prefer to defer this problem until make-or-buy decisions have been studied in Chapter 10.

Answer to question 4.1

Overhead absorbed (£714,000) = Actual hours (119,000) × Pre-determined overhead rate.

Pre-determined overhead rate = £714,000/119,000 = £6.

Budgeted overheads (£720,000) = Budgeted machine hours × Budgeted overhead rate (£6).

Budgeted machine hours = £720,000/£6 = 120,000 hours.

Answer = C

Answer to question 4.2

Budgeted overhead rate = £258,750/11,250 hours = £23 per machine hour.

Overheads absorbed = £23 × 10,980 Actual hours = £252,540.

Overheads incurred = £254,692

Overheads absorbed = £252,540

Under-absorbed overheads = £2,152

Answer = A

Answer to question 4.3(i)

Budgeted overhead rates and not actual overhead rates should be used as indicated in Chapter 4.

Overhead rate = £148,750/8,500 hours = £17.50 per hour.

Answer = A

Answer to question 4.3(ii)

	£
Actual overheads incurred	146,200
Overheads absorbed (7,928 × £17.50)	138,740
Under-absorbed overheads	7,460

Answer = D

Answer to question 4.4(i)

It is assumed that labour cost is to be used as the allocation base.

Total labour cost = £14,500 + £3,500 + £24,600 = £42,600.

Overhead recovery rate = £126,000/£42,600 = £2.9578 per £1 of labour.

Overhead charged to Job CC20 = £24,600 × £2.9578 = £72,761.

Answer = C

Answer to question 4.4(ii)

	£
Opening WIP	42,790
Direct labour	3,500
Overhead (£3,500 × £2.9578)	10,352
	56,642
Selling price (£56,642/0.667)	84,921
or £56,642 divided by ⅔ =	£84,963

Answer = C

Answer to question 4.4(iii)

closing WIP = Total cost of AA10 and CC20

	Total £	AA10 £	CC20 £
Opening WIP		26,800	0
Materials in period		17,275	18,500
Labour in period		14,500	24,600
Overheads in period:			
2.9577465 × £14,500		42,887	
2.9577465 × £24,600			72,761
	217,323	101,462	115,861

Answer = D

Answer to question 4.10

(a) Calculation of department overhead rates

	Department P £	Department Q £	Department R £
Repairs and maintenance	42,000	10,000	10,000
Depreciation	17,000[a]	14,000	9,000
Consumable supplies	4,500[b]	2,700	1,800
Wage related costs	48,250	26,250	12,500
Indirect labour	45,000	27,000	18,000
Canteen/rest/smoke room	15,000[c]	9,000	6,000
Business rates and insurance	13,000[d]	10,400	2,600
	184,750	99,350	55,900
Direct labour hours	50,000	30,000	20,000
Overhead absorption rate	£3.70	£3.31	£3.00

Notes:
The calculations for Department P are:
[a]Depreciation = £170,000/£400,000 × £40,000.
[b]Consumable supplies = 50,000/100,000 × £9,000.
[c]Canteen = 25/50 × £30,000.
[d]Business rates insurance = 5,000/10,000 × £26,000.

(b) Job 976: Sample quotation

		£	£
Direct materials			800.00
Direct labour	P (30 × £7.72[a])	231.60	
	Q (10 × £7.00[b])	70.00	
	R (5 × £5.00[c])	25.00	326.60
Overhead absorbed	P (30 × £3.70)	111.00	
	Q (10 × £3.31)	33.10	
	R (5 × £3.00)	15.00	159.10
Production cost			1,285.70
Selling, distribution and administration costs (20% × £1,285.70)			257.14
Total cost			1,542.84
Profit margin (20% of selling price)			385.71
Selling price (£1,542.84 × 100/800)			1,928.55

Notes:
[a]£386,000/50,000.
[b]£210,000/30,000.
[c]£100,000/20,000.

(c)

	£
Direct materials	800.00
Direct labour	326.60
Prime cost	1,126.60
Overhead applied (125%)	1,408.25
Total cost	2,534.85

The auditor's system results in a higher cost for this quotation. However, other jobs will be overcosted with the previous system. The auditor's system will result in the reporting of more accurate job costs with some job costs being higher, and others being lower, than the present system. For a more detailed answer see the section on blanket overhead rates in Chapter 4.

Answer to question 4.11

(a)
Departments

	Total	A	B	C	X	Y
	£	£	£	£	£	£
Rent and rates[a]	12,800	6,000	3,600	1,200	1,200	800
Machine insurance[b]	6,000	3,000	1,250	1,000	500	250
Telephone charges[c]	3,200	1,500	900	300	300	200
Depreciation[b]	18,000	9,000	3,750	3,000	1,500	750
Supervisors' salaries[d]	24 000	12,800	7,200	4,000		
Heat and light[a]	6,400	3,000	1,800	600	600	400
	70,400					
Allocated		2,800	1,700	1,200	800	600
		38,100	20,200	11,300	4,900	3,000
Reapportionment of X		2,450 (50%)	1,225 (25%)	1,225 (25%)	(4,900)	
Reapportionment of Y		600 (20%)	900 (30%)	1,500 (50%)		(3,000)
		£41,150	£22,325	£14,025		
Budgeted D.L. hours[c]		3,200	1,800	1,000		
Absorption rates		£12.86	£12.40	£14.02		

Notes:
[a] Apportioned on the basis of floor area.
[b] Apportioned on the basis of machine value.
[c] Should be apportioned on the basis of the number of telephone points or estimated usage. This information is not given and an alternative arbitrary method of apportionment should be chosen. In the above analysis telephone charges have been apportioned on the basis of floor area.
[d] Apportioned on the basis of direct labour hours.
[c] Machine hours are not given but direct labour hours are. It is assumed that the examiner requires absorption to be on the basis of direct labour hours.

(b)	Job 123	Job 124
	£	£
Direct material	154.00	108.00
Direct labour:		
Department A	76.00	60.80
Department B	42.00	35.00
Department C	34.00	47.60
Total direct cost	306.00	251.40
Overhead:		
Department A	257.20	205.76
Department B	148.80	124.00
Department C	140.20	196.28
Total cost	852.20	777.44
Profit	284.07	259.15
(c) Listed selling price	1,136.27	1,036.59

Note:
Let SP represent selling price.
Cost + 0.25SP = SP
Job 123: £852.20 + 0.25SP = 1SP
$\quad\quad\quad\quad$ 0.75 SP = £852.20
$\quad\quad\quad\quad$ Hence SP = £1,136.27
For Job 124: $\quad$ 0.75SP = £777.44
$\quad\quad\quad\quad$ Hence SP £1,036.59

(d) For the answer to this question see the section on material control procedure in Chapter 3.

Answer to question 4.13

(a) Overhead analysis sheet for ABC Limited for the year ending 31 December 1995

Expense	Machining £000	Assembly £000	Finishing £000	Maintenance £000	Total £000	Basis of apportionment
Indirect wages	10	6	8	30	54	Allocation
Indirect material	15	4	8	20	47	Allocation
Power	80	10	12	–	102	Machine hours
Light and heat	5	2	1.5	1.5	10	Area
Depreciation	4	1.6	0.6	0.8	7	Book value
Rent and rates	12.5	5	3.75	3.75	25	Area
Personnel	18	12	24	9	63	No. of employees
	144.5	40.6	57.85	65.05	308	
Reallotment of maintenance	39.03	13.01	13.01	(65.05)	–	
	183.53	53.61	70.86	–	308	

(b)

Machining $\dfrac{£183,530}{40,000 \text{ hours}}$ <u>£4.59</u> per machine hour

Assembly $\dfrac{£53,610}{8,000 \text{ hours}}$ <u>£6.70</u> per direct labour hour

Finishing $\dfrac{£70,860}{16,000 \text{ hours}}$ <u>£4.43</u> per direct labour hour

Note that assembly and Finishing Department overheads are recovered on the basis of direct labour hours, since direct labour hours represent the predominant activity. In the Machining Department overheads are likely to be most closely related to machine hours.

(c) Cost estimate:

			£	£
Direct material (2,500 + 400 + 200)				3,100
Direct labour:	Machining	$\left(800 \text{ hrs} \times \dfrac{£60,000}{12,000 \text{ hours}}\right)$	4,000	
	Assembly	$\left(350 \text{ hrs} \times \dfrac{£32,000}{8,000 \text{ hours}}\right)$	1,400	
	Finishing	$\left(140 \text{ hrs} \times \dfrac{£72,000}{16,000 \text{ hours}}\right)$	630	6,030

Production overheads:

			£	£
	Machining	1400×4.59	6,426	
	Assembly	350×6.70	2,345	
	Finishing	140×4.43	620.20	9,391.20
				18,521.20

(d) Machining department – fixed production overhead control account

	£		£
Creditors	128,000	WIP^a	179,010
Profit & Loss A/C (Over-recovery of overheads)	51,010		
	179,010		179,010

Note:
^{a} 39,000 machine hours × £4.59 per hour = £179,010.

(e)

	£		
Expenditure	55,530	favourable	[Budgeted cost (£183,530 − actual cost £128,000)]
Volume	4,520	adverse	(Balancing figure)
	51,010	favourable	

Answer to question 4.14

(a)

		£	£
Photography: 64 pages at £150 per page			9,600
Set-up:			
Labour – 64 plates × 4 hours per plate			
= 256 hours at £7 per hour		1,792	
Materials – 64 plates at £35 per plate		2,240	
Overhead – 256 labour hours at £9.50 per hour		2,432	
			6,464

Printing:
  Materials (paper):

$$100,000 \text{ catalogues} \times 32 \text{ sheets} \times \frac{£12}{1,000} \times \frac{100}{98} \qquad 39,184$$

Materials (other):
$$\frac{100,000}{500} \times £7 \qquad\qquad\qquad 1,400$$

Labour and Overheads –
$$\frac{100,000}{1,000} \text{ m/c hours at £62 per hour} \qquad 6,200$$

$$\qquad\qquad\qquad\qquad\qquad\qquad 46,784$$

Binding:
Labour and Overheads –
$$\frac{100,000}{2,500} \text{ m/c hours at £43 per hour} \qquad 1,720$$

Total costs $\qquad\qquad\qquad\qquad\qquad\qquad 64,568$

Selling price – $£64,568 \times \dfrac{100}{90} \qquad\qquad 71,742$

(b) Estimated hours = 256

Actual hours = $256 \times \dfrac{100}{90}$

$\qquad\qquad = 284.4$

Additional costs = $(284.4 - 256) \times £16.50$ (£7 labour rate + £9.50 overhead rate)

$\qquad\qquad\qquad = £469.3$

Answer to question 4.16

(a) Percentage of direct material cost $= \dfrac{£250,000}{£100,000} \times 100 = 250\%$

Direct labour hour rate = £250,000/50,000 hours = £5 per hour

(b) Percentage material cost = 250% × £7,000 = £17,500
Direct labour cost $\qquad$ = 800 × £5 = £4,000

(c) Overhead incurred £350,000
Overhead absorbed £275,000 (55,000 × £5)
Under-absorption of overhead £75,000
The under-absorption of overhead should be regarded as a period cost and charged to the profit and loss account.

(d) The answer should stress the limitations of the percentage of direct material cost method and justify why the direct labour hour method is the most frequently used method in non-machine paced environments. See Appendix 4.2 for a more detailed answer to this question.

Answer to question 4.18

(a) *Year 1:*
    (1) Budgeted machine hours   132,500
    (2) Budgeted fixed overheads   £2,411,500 (132,500 × £18.20)
    (3) Actual machine hours   134,200 (£2,442,440/£18.20)

(4) Fixed overheads absorbed   £2,442,440
(5) Actual fixed overheads incurred   £2,317,461

   Over-absorption of fixed overheads   £124,979 (5 − 4)

The section on under- and over-recovery of fixed overheads in Chapter 4 indicates that an under- or over-recovery will arise whenever actual activity or expenditure differs from budgeted activity or expenditure. Actual activity was 1,700 hours in excess of budget and this will result in an over-recovery of fixed overheads of £30,940. Actual overheads incurred were £94,039 (£2,317,461 − £2,411,500) less than budget and this is the second factor explaining the over-absorption of fixed overheads.

Summary:	£
Over-recovery due to actual expenditure being less than budgeted expenditure	94,039
Over-recovery due to actual activity exceeding budgeted activity	30,940
Total over-recovery of overhead for year 1	124,979

Year 2:
(1) Budgeted machine hours (134,200 × 1.05)	140,910
(2) Budgeted fixed overheads	£2,620,926
(3) Fixed overhead rate (£2,620,926/140,900 hours)	£18.60
(4) Actual fixed overheads incurred	£2,695,721
(5) Fixed overheads absorbed (139,260 × £18.60)	£2,590,236
(6) Under-recovery of overhead for year 2 (4 − 5)	£105,485

Analysis of under-recovery of overhead:	£
Under-recovery due to actual activity being less than activity (139,260 − 140,910) × £18.60	30,690
Under-recovery due to actual expenditure being greater than budgeted expenditure (£2,695,721 − £2,620,926	74,795
Total under-recovery for the year	105,485

Change in the overhead rate:
Change in the rate (£18.60 − £18.20)/£18.20	=	+ 2.198%
This can be analysed as follows:		
Increase in budgeted expenditure (£2,620,926 − £2,411,500)/£2,411,500	=	+ 8.684%
Increase in budgeted activity (140,910 hours − 132,500 hrs)/132,500	=	+ 6.347%

The increase of 2.198% in the absorption rate is due to an expenditure increase of 8.684% in budgeted expenditure partly offset by an increase in budgeted activity of 6.347% over the 2 years.

Proof:
(1.08684/1.06347) − I = 0.02198 (2.198%)

(b) See the sections on blanket and departmental overhead rates and pre-determined overhead rates in Chapter 4 for the answers to these questions.

Answer to question 4.21

(a) (i) and (ii) An activity increase of 150 hours (1,650 − 1,500) results in an increase in total overheads of £675. It is assumed that the increase in total overheads is due entirely to the increase in variable overheads arising from an increase in activity. Therefore the variable overhead rate is £4.50 (£675/150 hours) per machine hour. The cost structure is as follows:

1. Activity level (hours)	1,500	1,650	2,000
2. Variable overheads at £4.50 per hour	£6,750	£7,425	£9,000
3. Total overheads	£25,650	£26,325	£27,900
4. Fixed overheads (3 − 2)	£18,900	£18,900	£18,900

(iii) The fixed overhead rate is £10.50 (£15 − £4.50 variable rate)

Normal activity = Fixed overheads (£18,900)/Fixed overhead rate (£10.50)
= 1,800 machine hours

(iv) Under-absorption = 100 machine hours (1,800 − 1,700) at £10.50 = £1,050

(b) (i) A machine hour rate is recommended for the machine department because most of the overheads (e.g. depreciation and maintenance) are likely to be related to machine hours. For non-machine labour-intensive departments, such as the finishing department, overheads are likely to be related to direct labour hours rather than machine hours. Overheads are therefore charged to jobs performed in the finishing department using the direct labour hour method of recovery.

Calculation of overhead rates:

	Machining department	Finishing department
Production overhead	£35,280	£12,480
Machine hours	11,200	
Direct labour hours		7,800
Machine hour overhead rate	£3.15	
Direct labour hour overhead rate		£1.60

(ii)

	Machining department £	Finishing department £
Direct materials		
(189 × 1.1 × £2.35/0.9)	542.85	–
Direct labour[a]		
25 hours × £4	100.00	
28 hours × £4		112.00
Production overhead		
46 machine hours at £3.15	144.90	
28 direct labour hours at £1.60		44.80
	787.75	156.80

Total cost of job = £944.55 (£787.75 + £156.80)

Note:
[a] Overtime premiums are charged to overheads, and are therefore not included in the above job cost.

Answer to question 4.23

(a)   (i) *Calculation of budgeted overhead absorption rates:*

Apportionment of overheads to production departments

	Machine shop £	Fitting section £	Canteen £	Machine maintenance section £	Total £
Allocated overheads	27,660	19,470	16,600	26,650	90,380
Rent, rates, heat and light[a]	9,000	3,500	2,500	2,000	17,000
Depreciation & insurance of equipment[a]	12,500	6,250	2,500	3,750	25,000
	49,160	29,220	21,600	32,400	132,380
Service department apportionment					
Canteen[b]	10,800	8,400	(21,600)	2,400	–
Machine maintenance section	24,360	10,440	–	(34,800)	–
	84,320	48,060	–	–	132,380

Calculation of absorption bases:

		Machine shop			Fitting section	
Product	Budgeted production	Machine hours per product	Total machine hours		Direct labour cost per product	Total direct wages
X	4,200 units	6	25,200		12	50,400
Y	6,900 units	3	20,700		3	20,700
Z	1,700 units	4	6,800		21	35,700
			52,700			106,800

Budgeted overhead absorption rates:

Machine shop

$$\frac{\text{Budgeted overheads}}{\text{Budgeted machine hours}} = \frac{£84,320}{52,700}$$

$$= £1.60 \text{ per machine hour}$$

Fitting section

$$\frac{\text{Budgeted overheads}}{\text{Budgeted direct wages}} = \frac{£48,060}{£106,800}$$

$$= 45\% \text{ of direct wages}$$

Notes:

[a] Rent, rates. heat and light are apportioned on the basis of floor area. Depreciation and insurance of equipment are apportioned on the basis of book value.

[b] Canteen costs are reapportioned according to the number of employees. Machine maintenance section costs are reapportioned according to the percentages given in the question.

(ii) The budgeted manufacturing cost for producing one unit of product X is as follows:

	£
Machine shop: 6 hours at £1.60 per hour	9.60
Fittings section: 45% of £12	5.40
	15.00

(b) The answer should discuss the limitations of blanket overhead rates and actual overhead rates. See sections on blanket overhead rates and departmental overhead rates and predetermined overhead rates in Chapter 4 for the answer to this question.

Answer to question 4.24

(a) The service department cost should be reallocated using the following bases:
Canteen: Number of employees
Engineering shop: Number of service hours
Stores: Number of stores orders
The canteen does not receive any services from the other service departments. Therefore the canteen should be reallocated first. The Engineering Shop receives services from the other two service departments and should be reallocated last.

Dept.	Basis	M/C	Assemb	Paint	Eng shop	Stores shop	Canteen
		£	£	£	£	£	£
Allocation		180,000	160,000	130,000	84,000	52,000	75,000
Canteen	Employees	27,000	17,000	13,000	10,000	8,000	(75,000)
Stores	Orders	24,000	18,000	12,000	6,000	(60,000)	
Eng. shop	Service hrs	45,000	30,000	25,000	(100,000)		
Total overhead		276,000	225,000	180,000			
Machine hours		9,200					
Direct labour hours			11,250				
Labour cost				£45,000			
Machine hour rate		£30					
Direct labour hour rate		£20					
Direct labour cost rate		400% of direct labour cost					

(b) *Overhead absorption statement:*

	Machine	Assembly	Paint shop
	£	£	£
Overhead absorbed[a]	300,000	156,000	140,000
Actual overhead	290,000	167,000	155,000
(Under-) Over-absorption	10,000	11,000	15,000

Notes:
[a] 10,000 machine hours × £30 per hour.
7,800 Direct labour hours at £20 per hour.
400% of direct labour cost of £35,000.

(c) See the section on predetermined overhead rates in Chapter 4 for an explanation of why overheads should be absorbed using predetermined bases. The second part of the question relates to whether or not volume allocation base (i.e. machine hours and direct labour hours or cost) are appropriate, particularly when direct labour is a small proportion of total cost. The answers should discuss the need for developing non-volume-based cost driver rates using activity-based costing systems. Activity-based costing is described in Chapter 11.

Answer to question 4.25

(a) To calculate product cost, we must calculate overhead absorption rates for the production departments. You can see from the question that the service departments serve each other, and it is therefore necessary to use the repeated distribution method or the simultaneous equation method to reallocate the service department costs. Both methods are illustrated below:

	Cutting £	Machining £	Pressing £	Engineering £	Personnel £
Allocation per question	154,482	64,316	58,452	56,000	34,000
Engineering reallocation	11,200(20%)	25,200(45%)	14,000(25%)	(56,000)	5,600(10%)
Personnel reallocation	21,780(55%)	3,960(10%)	7,920(20%)	5,940(15%)	(39,600)
Engineering reallocation	1,188(20%)	2,673(45%)	1,485(25%)	(5,940)	594(10%)
Personnel reallocation	327(55%)	59(10%)	119(20%)	89(15%)	(594)
Engineering reallocation[a]	20	44	25	(89)	
	188,997	96,252	82,001	–	–

Note:
[a]The costs are so small that any further apportionments are not justified. Consequently a return charge of 15% is not made to the engineering department and the costs are apportioned in the ratio 55:10:20.

Simultaneous equation method:
Let
E = total overhead allocated to engineering department
and
P = total overhead allocated to personnel department
Then
$E = 56,000 + 0.15P$
$P = 34,000 + 0.10E$

Rearranging the above equations,

$$E - 0.15P = 56,000 \quad (1)$$
$$-0.10E + P = 34,000 \quad (2)$$

Multiplying equation (2) by 0.15 and equation (1) by 1,

$$E - 0.15P = 56,000$$
$$-0.015E + 0.15P = 5,100$$

Adding these equations,

$$0.985E = 61,100$$
$$E = £62,030$$

and so

Substituting for E in equation (1),

$$62,030 - 0.15P = 56,000$$
$$6,030 = 0.15P$$
$$P = 40,200$$

and so

We now apportion the values of E and P to the production departments in the agreed percentages:

	Cutting £	Machining £	Pressing £
Allocation per question	154,482	64,316	58,452
Allocation of engineering	12,408(20%)	27,914(45%)	15,508(25%)
Allocation of personnel	22,110(55%)	4,020(10%)	8,040(20%)
	189,000	96,250	82,000

Overhead absorption rates:
A comparison of the machine and direct labour hours in the machine department indicates that machine hours are the dominant activity. Therefore a machine hour rate should be used. A direct labour hour rate is appropriate for the cutting and pressing departments. Note that unequal wage rates apply in the cutting department, but equal wage rates apply in the pressing department. The direct wages percentage and the direct labour hour methods will therefore result in identical overhead charges to products passing through the pressing department, and either method can be used. Because of the unequal wage rates in the cutting department, the direct wages percentage method is inappropriate.

The calculation of the overhead absorption rates are as follows:

		(hours)
Cutting:	Product A (4,000 × 9 hours)	36,000
	Product B (3,000 × 6 hours)	18,000
	Product C (6,000 × 5 hours)	30,000
	Total	84,000

$$\text{Absorption rate} = \frac{£189,000}{84,000} = £2.25 \text{ per direct labour hour}$$

Machining:	Product A (4,000 × 2)	8,000
	Product B (3,000 × $1\frac{1}{2}$)	4,500
	Product C (6,000 × $2\frac{1}{2}$)	15,000
		27,500

$$\text{Absorption rate} = \frac{\text{\pounds}96{,}250}{27{,}500} = \text{\pounds}3.50 \text{ per direct labour hour}$$

Pressing:		
	Product A (4,000 × 2)	8,000
	Product B (3,000 × 3)	9,000
	Product C (6,000 × 4)	24,000
		41,000

$$\text{Absorption rate} = \frac{\text{\pounds}82{,}000}{41{,}000} = \text{\pounds}2 \text{ per direct labour hour}$$

Product cost calculations:

		A (fully complete)	B (partly complete)
	£	£	£
Direct materials		7.00	4.00
Direct labour: Cutting (Skilled)		12.00 (3 × £4)	20.00 (5 × £4)
(Unskilled)		15.00 (6 × £2.50)	2.50 (1 × £2.50)
Machining		1.50 ($\frac{1}{2}$ × £3)	0.75 ($\frac{1}{4}$ × £3)
Pressing		6.00 (2 × £3)	–
Prime cost		41.50	27.25
Overhead: Cutting		20.25 (9 × £2.25)	13.50 (6 × £2.25)
Machining		7.00 (2 × £3.50)	5.25 (1$\frac{1}{2}$ × £3.50)
Pressing		4.00 (2 × £2)	–
		72.75	46.00
		a(i)	a(ii)

(b) The accounting entries for overheads are presented in Chapter 5. You will find when you read this chapter that a credit balance in the overhead control account represents an over-recovery of overheads. Possible reasons for this include:

(i) actual overhead expenditure was less than budgeted expenditure;

(ii) actual production activity was greater than budgeted production activity.

Accounting entries for a job costing system

Answers to Chapter 5

Question summary

5.1 and 5.2
Preparation of ledger accounts for an integrated accounting system.

5.6 to 5.8
Preparation of ledger accounts for an interlocking accounting system. Question 5.7 also includes a reconciliation of the cost accounts with the financial accounts and 5.8 requires the preparations of accounts from incomplete information.

5.9 and 5.10
Reconciliation of the cost and financial accounts.

5.11
Preparation of cost ledger accounts where extracts from the financial accounts and the reconciliation of the costing and financial accounting profit are given in the question.

5.12
Stores pricing on a weighted average basis and the preparation of the raw materials and finished goods accounts.

5.13 and 5.14
Preparation of journal entries for payroll and labour cost accounting.

5.15 and 5.16
Preparation of the wages control accounts. Question 5.15 also requires the analysis of gross wages and the preparation of the overhead control account.

5.17 and 5.20
Preparation of contract accounts.

Answer to question 5.1

Where substantial costs have been incurred on a contract and it is nearing completion the following formula is often used to determine the attributable profit to date:

$$2/3 \times \text{Notional profit} \times \frac{\text{cash received}}{\text{value of work certified}}$$

$$= 2/3 \times (\pounds1.3\text{ m} - \pounds1\text{ m}) \times \pounds1.2\text{ m}/\pounds1.3\text{ m} = \pounds276,923$$

Answer = B

Answer to question 5.2

	Cost accounts	Financial accounts	Difference
Stock increase	£33,230	£15,601	£17,629

The stock increase shown in the cost accounts is £17,629 more than the increase shown in the financial accounts. Closing stocks represent expenses to be deferred to future accounting periods. Therefore the profit shown in the cost accounts will be £176,129 (£158,500 + £17,629).

Answer = C

Answer to question 5.3

(a) The opening WIP balance indicates that overheads are absorbed as follows:

Process 1 = Production overhead (125)/Direct wages (50) = 250% of direct wages
Process 2 = Production overhead (105)/Direct wages (70) = 150% of direct wages

(b) NB Limited accounts (All figures in £000)

Building account

	£		£
Balance	800		

Plant account

	£		£
Balance	480		

Provision for depreciation – plant account

	£		£
Balance c/fwd	108	Balance b/fwd	100
		Production overhead control (96/12 months)	8
	108		108
		Balance b/fwd	108

Raw material stocks account

	£		£
Balance b/fwd	400	Creditors	10
Creditors	210	Work in progress 1	136
		Work in progress 2	44
		Balance c/fwd	420
	610		610
Balance b/fwd	420		

Work in Progress 1 account

	£		£
Balance b/fwd	246	Abnormal loss[a]	20
Raw material stock	136	Work in progress 2b	483
Production overhead control	210	Balance c/fwd	173
($£84 \times 250\%$)			
Direct wages	84		
	676		676
Balance b/fwd	173		

Work in Progress 2 account

	£		£
Balance b/fwd	302	Finished goods[b]	908
Raw material stock	44	Abnormal loss[a]	33
Direct wages	130	Balance c/fwd	213
Production overhead control	195		
($£130 \times 150\%$)			
Work in progress 1	483		
	1,154		1,154
Balance b/fwd	213		

Finished goods account

	£		£
Balance b/fwd	60	Cost of sales	844
Work in progress 2	908	Balance c/fwd	124
	968		968
Balance b/fwd	124		

Debtors' account

	£		£
Balance b/fwd	1,120	Bank	1,140
Sales	1,100	Balance c/fwd	1,080
	2,220		2,220
Balance b/fwd	1,080		

Capital account

	£		£
		Balance b/fwd	2,200

Retained profit account

	£		£
		Balance	220

Creditors' account

	£		£
Raw material stocks	10	Balance b/fwd	300
Bank	330	Raw material stocks	210
Balance c/fwd	170		
	510		510
		Balance c/fwd	170

Bank account

	£		£
Debtors	1,140	Balance b/fwd	464
Balance c/fwd	466	Direct wages	200
		Production overhead control	170
		Production overhead control	250
		Creditors	330
		Administration overhead	108
		Selling/distribution overhead	84
	1,606		1,606
		Balance b/fwd	466

Sales account

	£		£
Balance c/fwd	2,300	Balance b/fwd	1,200
		Debtors	1,100
	2,300		2,300
		Balance b/fwd	2,300

Cost of sales account

	£		£
Balance b/fwd	888	Balance c/fwd	1,732
Finished goods	844		
	1,732		1,732
Balance b/fwd	1,732		

Abnormal loss account

	£		£
Balance b/fwd	9	Balance c/fwd	62
Work in progress 1[a]	20		
Work in progress 2[a]	33		
	62		62
Balance b/fwd	62		

Production overhead control account

	£		£
Bank	170		
Bank	250	Work in progress 1	210
Provision for depreciation	8	Work in progress 2	195
		Production overhead under/over-absorbed (Balance)	23
	428		428

Production overhead over-/under-absorbed account

	£		£
Production overhead control	23	Balance b/fwd	21
		Balance c/fwd	2
	23		23
Balance b/fwd	2		

Administration overhead account

	£		£
Balance b/fwd	120	Balance c/fwd	228
Bank	108		
	228		228
Balance b/fwd	228		

Selling and distribution overhead account

	£		£
Balance b/fwd	80	Balance c/fwd	164
Bank	84		
	164		164
Balance b/fwd	164		

Wages account

	£		£
Bank	200	Work in progress 1	84
Balance c/fwd	14	Work in progress 2	130
	214		214
		Balance b/fwd	14

Notes:

[a] The total cost of the abnormal losses are:

	Process 1	Process 2
	£	£
Direct materials	6	18
Direct wages	4	6
Production overhead	10 (250% × £4)	9 (150% × £6)
	20	33

[b] WIP transfers are:

	From WIP1 to WIP2	From WIP2 to Finished goods
	£	£
Direct materials	154	558
Direct wages	94	140
Production overhead	235 (250% × £94)	210 (150% × 140)
	483	908

(c) See the section on normal and abnormal losses in Chapter 6 for an explanation and possible reasons for abnormal losses.

Answer to question 5.5

(a) *Workings:*

Fixed overhead absorption rate   = £301,352/27,100 machine hours
   = £11.12 per machine hour
Variable overhead absorption rate = £96,021/£227,000
   = £0.423 per £ of direct labour
Fixed overheads absorbed   26,240 × £11.12 = £291,789
Variable overheads absorbed   = £212,630 × £0423 = £89,942

Direct materials stock

	£		£
Opening balance	97,260	WIP: issues	417,264
WIP: returns	13,118	Materials suppliers: returns	8,263
Materials suppliers:		Stock deficit (balance)	521
purchases	413,990	Closing balance	98,320
	524,368		524,368

Manufacturing overheads

	£		£
Suppliers: variable	90,672	WIP: variable overhead	
Suppliers: fixed	300,876	absorbed	89,942
		WIP: fixed overhead	
		absorbed	291,789
		Variable overhead under-	
		absorbed: P&L A/c	730
		Closing balance	9,087
	391,548		391,548

Work in progress

	£		£
Opening balance	15,668	Direct materials stock:	
Direct materials stock:		returns	13,118
issues	417,264	Completed production: to	
Direct labour	212,630	P&L A/c (balance)	991,462
Variable overhead absorbed	89,942	Closing balance	22,713
Fixed overhead absorbed	291,789		
	1,027,293		1,027,293

Materials suppliers (creditors)

	£		£
Bank: payments	389,761	Opening balance	56,473
Direct materials stock:		Direct materials stock:	
returns	8,263	purchases	413,990
Closing balance	72,439		
	470,463		470,463

(b) | | £ |
|---|---|
| Sales | 1,374,260 |
| Less cost of sales: | |
| Production costs | 991,462 |
| Direct materials stock deficit | 521 |
| Variable overhead under-absorption | 730 |
| Selling and administration overheads | 307,264 |
| | 1,299,977 |
| Net profit | 74,283 |

Answer to question 5.7

(a)   *Raw materials stores account*

	£		£
Balance b/d	49, 500	Work in progress	104,800
Purchases	108,800	Loss due to flood to P&L a/c	2,400
		Balance c/d	51,100
	£158,300		£158,300
Balance b/d	51,100		

Work in progress control account

	£		£
Balance b/d	60,100	Finished goods	222,500
Raw materials	104,800	Balance c/d	56,970
Direct wages	40,200		
Production overhead	74,370		
	£279,470		£279,470
Balance b/d	56,970		

Finished goods control account

	£		£
Balance b/d	115,400	Cost of sales	212,100
Work in progress	222,500	Balance c/d	125,800
	£337,900		£337,900
Balance b/d	125,800		

Production overhead

	£		£
General ledger control	60,900	Work in progress	
Notional rent (3 × £4,000)	12,000	(185% × £40,200)	74,370
Overhead over absorbed	1,470		
	£74 370		£74,370

General ledger control account

	£		£
Sales	440,000	Balance b/d (49,500 +	
Balance c/d	233,870	60,100 + 115,400)	225,000
		Purchases	108,800
		Direct wages	40,200
		Production overhead	60,900
		Notional rent	12,000
		P & L a/c	226,970
		(profit for period: see (b))	
	673,870		673,870

(b)   Calculation of profit in cost accounts:

	£	£
Sales		440,000
Cost of sales	212,100	
Loss of stores	2,400	
	214,500	
Less overhead over absorbed		
Profit	1,470	213,030
		226,970

Reconciliation statement:[a]

	£	£	£
Profit as per cost accounts			226,970
Differences in stock values:			
Raw materials opening stock	1,500		
Raw materials closing stock	900		
WIP closing stock	1,030	3,430	
WIP opening stock	3,900		
Finished goods opening stock	4,600		
Finished goods closing stock	3,900	(12,400)	(8,970)
Add items not included in financial accounts:			
Notional rent			12,000
Profit as per financial accounts			230,000

Note:
[a] Stock valuations in the financial accounts may differ from the valuation in the cost accounts. For example, raw materials may be valued on a LIFO basis in the cost accounts, whereas FIFO or weighted average may be used in the financial accounts. WIP and finished stock may be valued on a marginal (variable costing) basis in the cost accounts, but the valuation may be based on an absorption costing basis in the financial accounts. To reconcile the

ACCOUNTING ENTRIES FOR A JOB COSTING SYSTEM

profits, you should start with the profit from the cost accounts and consider what the impact would be on the profit calculation if the financial accounting stock valuations were used. If the opening stock valuation in the financial accounts exceeds the valuation in the cost accounts then adopting the financial accounting stock valuation will reduce the profits. If the closing stock valuation in the financial accounts exceeds the valuation in the cost accounts then adopting the financial accounting stock valuation will increase profits. Note that the notional rent is not included in the financial accounts and should therefore be deducted from the costing profit in the reconciliation statement.

(c) The over-recovery of overhead could be apportioned between cost of goods sold for the current period and closing stocks. The justification for this is based on the assumption that the under-/over-recovery is due to incorrect estimates of activity and overhead expenditure, which leads to incorrect allocations being made to the cost of sales and closing stock accounts. The proposed adjustment is an attempt to rectify this incorrect allocation.

The alternative treatment is for the full amount of the under-/over-recovery to be written off to the cost accounting profit and loss account in the current period as a period cost. This is the treatment recommended by SSAP 9.

Answer to question 5.9

Interlocking accounts reconciliation:

		£	£
Profit per accounts			75,000
Add back	Debenture interest	13,000	
	Write off of goodwill	20,000	
	Discounts allowed	7,000	
	Overheads	20,000	
			60,000
Less	Rent received	25,000	
	Notional rent	14,000	
	Discounts received	5,000	
	Profit on machine	6,000	
			(50,000)
Stock adjustments	Raw materials	2,000	
	Finished goods	6,000	
			8,000
Profit as per cost accounts			93,000

Answer to question 5.11

(a) (i)   *Raw materials stock account*

	£		£
Opening stock (110 − 7)	103	Issues (difference)	578
Purchases	640	Returns (to supplier)	20
		Closing stock (130 + 15)	145
	743		743

(ii)   *Work in progress account*

	£		£
Opening stock (25 + 3)	28	Finished goods a/c (difference)	984
Raw materials a/c	578	Closing stock (27 − 5)	22
Direct labour (220 + 20)	240		
Production overhead absorbed			
(240 at $66\frac{2}{3}\%$)	160		
	1,006		1,006

(iii)   *Finished goods account*

	£		£
Opening stock (82 − 9)	73	Cost of sales a/c (difference)	989
Work in progress a/c	984	Closing stock (72 − 4)	68
	1,057		1,057

(iv)   *Profit and loss account*

	£		£
Sales returns a/c	30	Sales a/c	1,530
Cost of sales a/c	989		
Gross profit c/d	511		
	1,530		1,530
Production overheads under-		Gross profit b/d	511
absorbed	2		
Administration expenses	200		
Net profit	309		
	511		511

The reconciliation statement indicates that discounts, selling expenses and debenture interest are not included in the cost accounts. Therefore these items are not included in the costing profit and loss account.

(b) Interest on capital tied up in stocks should be taken into account for decision-making and cost control purposes. This is because the interest on capital tied up in stocks represents an opportunity cost (in terms of the lost interest) which would have been earned if the money tied up in stocks had been invested.

Interest on capital tied up in stocks should not be included in product costs for stock valuation purposes per SSAP 9. Therefore the cost accumulation system will not include notional costs for stock valuation purposes. Nevertheless it is essential that all *relevant* costs (including opportunity costs) are included in cost statements for the purpose of decision-making and cost control.

Answer to question 5.12

(a) *Stores ledger card:*

Date		Kilos	Total value £	Average price per kilo £	
Opening balance		21,600	28,944	1.34	
1	Issue	(7,270)	(9,742)	1.34	
7	Purchase	17,400	23,490		
		31,730	42,692	1.3455	(£42,692/31,730)
8	Issue	(8,120)	(10,925)	1.3455	
15	Issue	(8,080)	(10,872)	1.3455	
20	Purchase	19,800	26,730		
		35,330	47,625	1.348	(£47,625/35,330)
22	Issue	(9,115)	(12,287)	1.348	
Closing balance		26,215	35,338	1.348	

Summary of transactions:

	£
Opening balance	28,944
Purchases	50,220
Issues	(43,826)
Closing balance	35,338

Raw material stock control account

	£		£
Opening balance	28,944	WIP	43,826
Purchases	50,220	Closing balance	35,338
	79,164		79,164

Production costs for the period:	£
Raw materials	43,826
Labour and overhead	35,407
	79,233

Cost per unit (£79,233/17,150 units)   £4.62

Units sold = opening stock (16,960) + production (17,150)
  − closing stock (17,080) = 17,030 units

Finished goods stock control account

	£		£
Opening balance	77,168	Cost of sales	
Raw materials	43,826	(difference/balancing figure)	77, 491
Labour and overhead	35,407	Closing balance	
		(17,080 × (£4.62)	78,910
	156,401		156,401

(b)   The financial ledger control account is sometimes described as a cost control account or a general ledger adjustment account. For an explanation of the purpose of this account see the section on interlocking accounting in Chapter 5.

(c)   *Budgeted production (units):*

Sales	206,000
Add closing stock	18,128 $(206,000 \times 1.10 \times 20/250)$
Less opening stock	(17,080)
	207,048 units

For month 12 the raw material usage is 1.90 kilos per unit of output:
$(7,270 + 8,120 + 8,080 + 9,115 = 32,585$ kg used$)/17,150$ units produced
∴ Budgeted material usage $= 207,048$ units $\times 1.9$ kg per unit
$= 393,391$ kg

Budgeted material purchases:

Budgeted usage	393,391 kg
Add closing stock	22,230 $(11,700 \times 1.9)$
Less opening stock	(26,215)
	389,406 kg

Answer to question 5.13

(a)   A wages control account is a summary account which records total wages payable including employers' national insurance contributions. The account is cleared by a credit and corresponding debits in respect of total wages costs charged to WIP and the overhead control account. The detail which supports the control account is maintained in subsidiary payroll records.

(b)   (i)

	Dr £	Cr £
Wages control	122,300	
Bank		122,300
Wages control	58,160	
Employees' National Insurance		14,120
Employees' pension fund contributions		7,200
Income tax		27,800
Court order retentions		1,840
Trade union subscriptions		1,200
Private health plans		6,000
	180,460	180,460
Production overhead control Dr	18,770	
Employer's National Insurance		18,770
	18,770	18,770

(ii)

Work-in-progress control:		
Wages	77,460	
Overtime wages – direct	16,800	
Production overhead control:		
Overtime premium	9,000	
Shift premium	13 000	
Indirect wages	38,400	
Overtime wages – indirect	10,200	
Warehouse construction account	2,300	
Statutory sick pay	9,000	
Idle time	4,300	
Wages control		180,460
	180,460	180,460

Answer to question 5.15

(a) *Calculation of gross wages:*

	Direct workers			Indirect workers			Total
			£			£	£
Attendance time	2,640 × 5.00	=	13,200	940 × 4.00	=	3,760	
Overtime premium	180 × 200	=	360	75 × 1.60	=	120	
Group bonuses			2,840			710	
Gross wages			16,400			4,590	20,990

(b) *Analysis of gross wages:*

	Direct charge (to WIP)			Indirect charge to production overhead			Total
Attendance time:			£			£	£
Direct workers	2,515 × 5.00	=	12,575	125 × 5.00	=	625	
Indirect workers				940 × 4.00	=	3,760	
Overtime premium:							
Direct workers	72 × 2.00	=	144	108 × 2.00	=	216	
Indirect workers	30 × 1.60	=	48	45 × 1.60	=	72	
Group bonuses							
Direct workers						2,840	
Indirect workers						710	
			12,767			8,223	20,990

Wages control account

	£		£
Cost ledger control	20,990	Work in progress	12,767
(Gross wages)		Production overhead	8,223
	20,990		20,990

Production overhead control account:

	£
Wages control	8,223
Cost ledger control	1,865
(Employers' employment costs)	

Answer to question 5.17

(a)   (i)   *Contract account:*

	£000		£000
Plant	8,000	Plant c/fwd	3,500
Planning and survey fees	2,000	Materials returns	500
Materials	15,000	Materials c/fwd	400
Labour	8,000		
Labour on cost	1,000	Cost of work certified b/d	
Plant hire	3,500	(cost of sales)	37,065
Site costs:			
Rent and rates	156		
Salaries	1,200		
Head Office costs	750		
Direct expenses	1,804		
Labour c/fwd	55		
	41,465		41,465
Costs of sales c/d	37,065	Attributable sales revenue	50,000
Profit taken	12,935		
	50,000		50,000
Plant b/fwd	3,500		
Materials b/fwd	400		

(ii)   The contract is approximately half complete and the budgeted profit is £27 m. Therefore the estimated share of the profit *to date* is approximately £13.23 m (50/102 × £27 m). However, the profit *to date* as per the above account is £12.935 m, and it is considered prudent to incorporate a profit of £12.935 m in the accounts. It is assumed that no retention money has been retained. Consequently, it is inappropriate to reduce the profit based on the formula illustrated in Chapter 5.

(iii)   In view of the fact that the contract is only 50% complete, the prudence concept may be applied and only a proportion of the profit taken. Applying the formula illustrated in Chapter 5 the profit taken could be as follows:

$$\frac{2}{3} \times \text{estimated profit (£27,000)} \times \frac{\text{value of work certified (£50,000)}}{\text{value of contract (£102,000)}}$$

$$= £8,824$$

Other alternative approaches are appropriate for applying the prudence concept.

(b) Because of the considerable length of time that is taken to complete a contract, it is necessary to determine the profit to be attributed to each accounting period. Financial accounting normally recognizes revenue when the goods are delivered, but such an approach is inappropriate for long-term contracts, since profits on large contracts would not be reported until they were completed. The profit and loss account would not reflect a fair view of the profitability of the company during the year, but would show only the results of contracts that had been completed before the year end. To overcome this problem, it is preferable to take credit for ascertainable profit while contracts are in progress.

It is difficult to estimate accurately the total profit on the contract or the proportion of profit to date. SSAP 9 recommends that in determining the proportion of profit taken to date the judgement involved should be exercised with prudence, and caution should be applied so that the profit on the contract to date is not overstated.

Answer to question 5.18

(a) *Contract accounts (for the previous year):*

	MNO £000	PQR £000	STU £000		MNO £000	PQR £000	STU £000
Materials on site b/fwd			25	Wages accrued b/fwd		2	
Plant on site b/fwd		35	170	Plant control a/c		8	
Materials control a/c	40	99	180	Materials on site c/fwd	8		
Wages control a/c	20	47	110	Plant on site c/fwd	70		110
Subcontractors a/c			35	Prepayment c/fwd			15
Salaries	6	20	25	Cost of work not certified			
Plant control a/c	90	15		c/fwd			26
Wages accrued c/fwd		5		Cost of sales for current			
				period (balance)	82	221	416
Apportionment of							
construction services[a]	4	10	22				
	160	231	567		160	231	567
Cost of work certified b/fwd	82	221	416	Attributable sales revenue[c]	82	200	530
Profit taken this period[b]			114	Loss taken[b]		21	
	82	221	530		82	221	530
Cost of work not certified				Wages accrued b/fwd		5	
b/fwd			26				
Materials on site b/fwd	8						
Plant on site b/fwd	70		110				
Prepayment b/fwd			15				

Notes:

[a] Costs incurred by construction services department:

	£000
Plant depreciation (12 − 5)	7
Salaries	21
Wages paid	8
	36

Wages incurred by each department are:

	£000
MNO	20
PQR	50 (47 + 5 − 2)
STU	110
	180

The costs apportioned to each contract are:

	£000	
MNO	4	$\left(\dfrac{20}{180} \times £36 \right)$
PQR	10	$\left(\dfrac{50}{180} \times £36 \right)$
STU	22	$\left(\dfrac{110}{180} \times £36 \right)$

[b] See (b) (i) for calculation.

[c] Profit taken plus cost of sales for the current period or cost of sales less loss to date.

(b) (i) *Contract MNO*: Nil.

Contract PQR:

	£
Cost of contract to date (see part (a))	411,000
Value of work certified	390,000
Recommended loss to be written off	21,000

Contract STU:

	£
Cost of work certified	786,000
Cost of work not yet certified	26,000
Estimated costs to complete	138,000
Estimated cost of contract	950,000
Contract price	1,100,000
Anticipated profit	150,000

The profit taken to date is calculated using the following formula:

$$\frac{\text{cash received to date } (£950,000)}{\text{contract price } (£1,100,000)} \times \text{estimated profit from the contract } (£150,000)$$

= £129,545 (say £129,000)

The profit taken for the current period is £114,000, consisting of the profit to date of £129,000 less the profit previously transferred to the profit and loss account of £15,000.

(ii) *Contract MNO:* This contract is at a very early stage, and it is unlikely that the outcome can be reasonably foreseen. It is therefore prudent not to anticipate any profit at this stage.

Contract PQR: This contract has incurred a loss and, applying the prudence concept, this loss should be written off as soon as it is incurred.

Contract STU: Applying the prudence concept, a proportion of the profit

$$\frac{\text{cash received to date}}{\text{contract price}}$$

is recognized in this period. The proportion of profit that is recognized is arbitrary and very much a matter of opinion. Alternative apportionments applying the concept of prudence could have been applied.

Process costing

Answers to Chapter 6

Question summary

6.1 to 6.5
Multiple choice questions.

6.6
An essay problem related to process costing.

6.7 to 6.9
Preparation of process accounts when there is no opening or closing WIP. Consequently. the problem of equivalent production does not arise. These questions require the preparation of abnormal loss and gain accounts.

6.10 and 6.11
Preparation of process accounts requiring the calculation of equivalent production and cost per equivalent unit using the weighted average basis. Neither problem includes any normal or abnormal losses.

6.12 to 6.16
Calculation of equivalent production and cost per equivalent unit using the weighted average basis. These questions include losses in process which are charged only to completed production. Questions 6.13, 6.15 and 6.16 involve losses in process which generate sales revenue. Questions 6.15 and 6.16 are the most difficult questions.

6.17
Similar to Questions 6.12 to 6.16 but with losses in process apportioned between work in progress and completed production.

6.18 and 6.19
Question 6.18 involves loss in process detected on completion and 6.19 involves an abnormal gain.

6.20
Preparation of process accounts with normal and abnormal losses not requiring equivalent production calculations plus a description of weighted average and FIFO methods of stock valuation.

6.21 to 6.23

Calculation of cost per equivalent unit using the FIFO basis. All of these questions include losses in process. Question 6.22 is the most difficult question requiring the calculation of unit costs for both the weighted average and FIFO methods.

6.24

Cost control problem requiring the preparation of a performance report using equivalent production calculations.

Answer to question 6.1

	Cost £	Units completed	Normal loss equiv. units	Abnormal loss equiv. units	Total equiv. units	Cost per unit £
Materials	90,000	36,000	3,000 (100%)	1,000 (100%)	40,000	2.25
Conversion cost	70,200	36,000	2,250 (75%)	750 (75%)	39,000	1.80
						4.05

Cost of abnormal loss:

Materials	$1,000 \times £2.25$	=	£2,250
Conversion cost	$750 \times £1.80$	=	£1,350
			£3,600

Answer = A

Answer to question 6.2

Abnormal gain debited to process account and credited to abnormal gain account:

	£	
Materials ($160 \times £9.40$)	1,504	
Conversion cost ($160 \times 0.75 \times £11.20$)	1,344	
		2,848
Lost sales of scrap ($180 \times £2$)		(360)
Net cost credited to profit and loss account		2,528

Answer = C

Answer to question 6.3

Answer = D

Answer to question 6.4

Input = Opening WIP (2,000 units) + Material input (24,000) = 26,000
Output = Completed units (19,500) + Closing WIP (3,000) + Normal Loss (2,400) = 24,900
Abnormal Loss = 1,100 units (Balance of 26,000 − 24,900)

Equivalent units (FIFO)

	Completed units less Opening WIP equiv. units	Closing WIP equiv. units	Abnormal loss equiv. units	Total equiv. units
Materials	17,500 (19,500 − 2,000)	3,000 (100%)	1,100 (100%)	21,600
Conversion	18,700 (19,500 − 800)	1,350 (45%)	1,100 (100%)	21,150

It is assumed that losses are detected at the end of the process and that the answer should adopt the short-cut method and ignore the normal loss in the cost per unit calculations.

Answer = C

Answer to Question 6.5

Closing stock = Opening stock (Nil) + Input (13,500) − Completed units (11,750)
= 1,750 units

It is assumed that materials are fully complete (£5.75) and labour and overheads are partly complete (£2.50)

Value of closing stock = (1,750 × £5.75) + (1,750 × £2.50) = £14,437.50

Answer = B

Answer to question 6.9

(a) (i)

Process A account

	kg	£		kg	£	£
Direct material	2,000	10,000	Normal loss	400	0.50	200
Direct labour		7,200	Process B	1,400	18.575	26,005
Process costs		8,400	Abnormal loss	200	18.575	3,715
Overhead		4,320				
	2,000	29,920		2,000		29,920

Unit cost = (£29,920 − £200)/1,600 = £18.575

(ii)

Process B account

	kg	£		kg	£	£
Process A	1,400	26,005	Finished goods	2,620	21.75	56,989
Direct material	1,400	16,800	Normal loss	280	1.825	511
Direct labour		4,200	(10% × 2,800)			
Overhead		2,520				

Process costs		5,800		
		55,325		
Abnormal gain	100	2,175		
	2,900	57,500	2,900	57,500

Unit cost = (£55,325 − £511)/(2,800 − 280) = £21.75

(iii)   *Normal loss/gain account*

	kg	£		kg	£
Process A	400	200	Bank (A)	400	200
Process B	280	511	Abnormal gain (B)	100	182.5
			Bank (B)	180	328.5
	680	711		680	711

(iv)   *Abnormal loss/gain*

	£		£
Process A	3,715	Process B	2,175
Normal loss/gain (B)	182.5	Bank	100
		Profit & Loss	1,622.5
	3,897.5		3,897.5

(v)   *Finished goods*

	£
Process B	56,989

(iv)   *Profit and loss account (extract)*

	£
Abnormal loss/gain	1,622.5

Answer to question 6.10

(a)   Units completed = 8,250 − Closing WIP (1,600) = 6,650
Calculation of number of equivalent units produced:

	Completed units	Closing WIP	Total equivalent units
Previous process	6,650	1,600	8,250
Materials	6,650	1,600	8,250
Labour and overhead	6,650	960 (60%)	7,610

(b)

	£	Total equivalent units £	Cost per unit
Previous process cost	453,750	8,250	55
Materials	24,750	8,250	3
Labour and overheads	350,060	7,610	46
			104

(c)

Process account

	Units	£		Units	£
Input from previous			Finished goods[a]	6,650	691,600
process	8,250	453,750	Closing WIP[b]	1,600	136,960
Materials		24,750			
Labour and overheads		350,060			
	8,250	828,560		8,250	828,560

Note:
[a] Cost of completed production = 6,650 units × £104 = £691,600

			£
[b] Closing WIP: Previous process cost (1,600 × £55)	=	88,000
Materials (1,600 × £3)	=	4,800
Labour and overhead (960 × £46)	=	44,160
		136,960

(d) See the introduction to Chapter 7 and the section on accounting for by-products in Chapter 7 for the answer to this question,

Answer to question 6.11

(a)

Cleansing agent process account

	kg	£		kg	£
Ingredient A	2,000	1,600	Completed production	8,600	9,460
B	3,000	1,500	WIP c/fwd (1,170 + 516)	2,400	1,686
C	6,000	2,400			
Wages		3,764			
Overheads		1,882			
	11,000	11,146		11,000	11,146

Calculation of cost per unit:

	Total cost £	Completed units	Equivalent WIP(1)	Equivalent WIP(2)	Total equivalent units	Cost per unit £
Materials	5,500	8,600	600	1,800	11,000	0.50
Labour	3,764	8,600	360	450	9,410	0.40
Overheads	1,882	8,600	360	450	9,410	0.20
	11,146					1.10

			£		
WIP(1):	Materials	600 × £0.50 =	300		
	Labour	360 × £0.40 =	144		
	Overheads	360 × £0.20 =	72	516	
WIP(2):	Materials	1,800 × £0.50 =	900		
	Labour	450 × £0.40 =	180		
	Overheads	450 × £0.20 =	90	1,170	
Completed units: 8,600 × £1.10				9,460	
				11,146	

Note that 11,000 kg were put into the process and 8,600 kg were completed. Therefore the WIP is 2,400 kg consisting of two batches – one of 600 units 60% complete and the second of 1,800 units 25% complete.

(b) See Chapter 6 for definitions and an explanation of the accounting treatment of abnormal gains and equivalent units. See Chapter 7 for a definition of by-products. Note that income from by-products should be credited to the process account from which the by-product emerges.

Answer to question 6.14

(a) *Production statement:*

Input		Output	
Opening stock	3,400	Finished stock	36,000
Input	37,000	WIP	3,200
		Normal loss	1,200
	40,400		40,400

Cost statement:

	Opening stock	Current cost	Total cost	Completed units	Normal loss	WIP equivalent units	Total equivalent units	Cost per unit	WIP
	£	£	£	£	£	£		£	£
Materials	25,500	276,340	301,840	36,000	1,200	3,200	40,400	7.47	23,904
Conversion cost	30,600	336,000	366,600	36,000	1,200	1,600	38,800	9.45	15,120
			668,440					16.92	39,024

Normal loss (1200 × £16.92)	20,304	
Completed units (36,000 × £16.92)	609,112	629,416
		668,440

The question does not indicate at what stage in the production process the normal loss is detected. It is assumed that the normal loss is detected at the end of the production process, consequently it is not allocated to WIP. Therefore the total cost of production transferred to finished stock is £629,416.

If the short-cut method described in Chapter 6 is adopted and the normal loss equivalent units are excluded from the above unit cost calculations, the closing WIP valuation is £40,240 and the value of completed production is £628,200. This is equivalent to the following calculation, which apportions the normal loss between completed production and WIP on the basis of equivalent production:

	Completed production £	WIP £
Materials normal loss		
(1,200 × £7.47 = £8,964)	8,232 (36,000/39,200)	732 (3,200/39,200)
Conversion cost normal loss		
(1,200 × £9.45 = £11,340)	10,857 (36,000/37,600)	483 (1,600/37,600)
Normal loss allocation	19,089	1,215
WIP per cost statement		39,024
Completed production	609,112	
	628,201	40,239

(b) The following characteristics distinguish process costing from job costing:
  (i) The cost per unit of output with a process costing system is the average cost per unit, whereas job costing traces the actual cost to each individual unit of output.
  (ii) Job costing requires that a separate order and job number be used to collect the cost of each individual job.
  (iii) With a process costing system, each unit of output is similar, whereas with a job costing system each unit of output is unique and requires different amounts of labour, material and overheads.
  (iv) With a job costing system, costs are accumulated for each order and WIP is calculated by ascertaining the costs that have been accumulated within the accounting period. With a process costing system, costs are not accumulated for each order and it is necessary to use the equivalent production concept to value WIP.
  (v) With a process costing system, the allocation of costs to cost of goods sold and closing stocks is not as accurate, because each cost unit is not separately identifiable. Consequently WIP is estimated using the equivalent production concept.

Answer to question 6.17

Statement of input and output (units):

Input	£	Output	£
Opening WIP	1,200	Completed and transferred to	
Transferred in	4,000	finished stock	3,200
		Normal loss	520
		WIP (completed units)	500
		Uncompleted WIP (balance)	980
	5,200		5,200

It is not clear from the question at what point in the process the loss occurs. It is assumed that the WIP has just passed the inspection point and should be charged with a share of normal loss. By adopting the short-cut method and making no entry for normal losses in the cost per unit calculations, the normal loss is automatically apportioned between completed units and WIP. You could have also assumed that the loss was detected when the goods were completed and charge all of the loss to completed production. If the question does not specify when the loss occurs, you should assume that it occurs either at the end of the process or that the WIP has just passed the inspection point. It is assumed that additional materials are added at the start of the process.

Statement of cost per unit:

	Opening WIP £	Current cost £	Total cost £	Completed units (W1)	Equivalent uncompleted WIP	Equivalent total units	Cost per unit £
Materials (W2)	10,800	34,830	45,630	3,700	980	4,680	9.75
Conversion cost	14,040	68,503	82,543	3,700	490	4,190	19.70
			128,173				29.45

	£
WIP: Completed units (500 × £29.45)	14,725
Uncompleted units: Materials (980 × £9.75)	9,555
Conversion cost (490 × £19.70)	9,653
	33,933
Completed units transferred to finished stock (3,200 × £29.45)	94,240
	128,173

(*W1*) Completed units = 3,200 + 500 (Completed WIP)
(*W2*) Materials include previous process cost (4,000 units at £7.50 each is included in the current cost column).

Process account

	Units	£		Units	£
WIP b/fwd:	1,200		Normal loss	520	–
Materials		10,800	Transferred to		
Conversion cost		14,040	finished stock	3,200	94,240
Transferred from			Completed		
previous process	4,000	30,000	WIP c/fwd	500	14,725
Materials		4,830	Uncompleted		
Direct wages		32,965	WIP c/fwd	980	19,208
Overhead		35,538			
	5,200	128,173		5,200	128,173

Answer to question 6.18

(a) Fully complete production = Input (36,000) − Closing WIP (8,000)
    = 28,000 kg
Normal loss = 2,800 (10% × 28,000 kg)
Abnormal loss = 800 (Actual loss (3,600) − 2,800)
Good output = 24,400 (28,000 − 3,600)

(b)

		Completed units £	Normal loss	Abnormal loss	Closing WIP	Total equiv. units	Cost per unit £
Previous process cost	166,000	24,400	2,800	800	8,000	36,000	4.61111
Conversion cost	73,000	24,400	2,800	800	4,000	32,000	2.28125
	239,000						6.89236

		£	£
Completed units (24,400 × £6.89236)		168,174	
Add normal loss (2,800 × £6.89236)		19,298	
			187,472
Abnormal loss (800 × £6.89236)			5,514
WIP: Previous process cost (8,000 × £4.61111)		36,889	
Conversion cost (4,000 × £2.28125)		9,125	
			46,014
			239,000

The above computations assume that losses are detected at the end of the process when the units are fully complete. Therefore none of the normal loss is allocated to partly completed units (WIP). There is an argument for allocating the normal loss between completed units and the abnormal loss (See the section on equivalent units and abnormal losses in Chapter 6) but it is unlikely to make a significant difference to the answer. Also examination questions are unlikely to require such sophisticated answers.

An alternative approach is to adopt the short-cut method described in Chapter 6. This method allocates the normal loss between completed units, WIP and the abnormal loss. Because the units actually lost are fully complete it is likely that losses are detected on completion. Therefore the short-cut method is not theoretically correct. Nevertheless the computations suggest that it was the examiner's intention that the question should be answered using the short-cut method. The revised answer is as follows:

	£	Completed units	Abnormal loss	WIP	Total equiv. units	Cost per unit £	WIP £
Previous process cost	166,000	24,400	800	8,000	33,200	5.00	40,000
Conversion cost	73,000	24,400	800	4,000	29,200	2.50	10,000
	239,000					7.50	50,000

		£
Completed units (24,400 × £7.50)		183,000
Abnormal loss (800 × £7.50)		6,000
		239,000

Distillation Process Account

	kg	£		kg	£
Input from mixing	36,000	166,000	Finished goods	24,400	183,000
Labour		43,800	Abnormal loss	800	6,000
Overheads		29,200	Normal loss	2,800	–
			Closing WIP	8,000	50,000
	36,000	239,000		36,000	239,000

(c) If the scrapped production had a resale value the resale value would be credited to the process account (thus reducing the cost of the process account). The accounting entries would be as follows:

Dr Cash
Cr Process Account (with sales value of normal loss)
Cr Abnormal Loss Account (with sales value of abnormal loss)

Answer to question 6.20

(a) Expected output from an input of

39,300 sheets:	3,144,000 cans (39,300 × 80)
Less 1% rejects	31,440 cans
Expected output after rejects	3,112,560 cans

The normal loss arising from the rejects (31,440 cans) is sold at £0.26 per kg. It is therefore necessary to express the rejects in terms of kilos of metal. Each sheet weighs 2 kilos but wastage in the form of offcuts is 2% of input. Therefore the total weight of 80 cans is 1.96 kg (0.98 × 2 kg) and the weight of each can is 0.0245 kilos (1.96 kg/80 cans). The weight of the normal loss arising from the rejects is 770.28 kg (31,440 × 0.0245 kg). The normal loss resulting from the offcuts is 1,572 kg (39,300 × 2 kg × 0.02). Hence the total weight of the normal loss is 2,342.28 kilos (1,572 kg + 770.28 kg), with an expected sales value of £609 (2,342.28 kg × £0.26).

Process account

	£		£
Direct materials		Finished goods	
(39,300 × £2.50)	98,250	(3,100,760 cans × £0.042[a])	130,232
		Normal loss	609
Direct labour and		Abnormal loss	
overheads	33,087	(11,800 kg[b] at £0.042[a])	496
	131,337		131,337

Abnormal loss account

	£		£
Process account	496	Sale proceeds[c]	75
		Profit and loss account	421
	496		496

Notes:

[a] Cost per unit = $\dfrac{£98,250 + £33,087 - £609}{\text{expected output (3,112,560 cans)}}$ = £0.042 per can

^{b} Expected output (3,112,560) – actual output (3 100,760 cans) = 11,800 cans
^{c} Abnormal loss = 11,800 cans (3 112,560 − 3,100,760)

This will yield 289.1 kilos (11,800 × 0.0245 kilos) of metal with a sales value of £75 (289.1 × £0.26).

(b)   (i) See the section on opening and closing work in progress in Chapter 6 for the answer to this question.

(ii) See the sections on weighted average method and first in, first out method in Chapter 6 for the answer to this question.

Answer to question 6.21

(a) *Production statement:*

Input:	Units
Opening WIP	20,000
Transfer from previous process	180,000
	200,000
Output:	
Closing WIP	18,000
Abnormal loss	60
Completed units (balance)	181,940
	200,000

Statement of equivalent production and calculation of cost of completed production and WIP:

	Current costs £	Completed units less opening WIP equivalent units	Abnormal loss	Closing WIP equivalent units	Current total equivalent units	Cost per unit £
Previous process cost	394,200	161,940	60	18000	180,000	2.19
Materials	110,520	167,940	60	16,200	184,200	0.60
Conversion cost	76,506	173,940	60	12,600	186,600	0.41
	581,226					3.20

	£	£
Cost of completed production:		
Opening WIP (given)	55,160	
Previous process cost (161,940 × £2.19)	354,649	
Materials (167,940 × £0.60)	100,764	
Conversion costs (173,940 × £0.41)	71,315	581,888
Cost of closing WIP:		
Previous process cost (18,000 × £2.19)	39,420	
Materials (16,200 × £0.60)	9,720	
Conversion costs (12,600 × £0.41)	5,166	54,306
Value of abnormal loss (60 × £3.20)		192
		636,386

Process 3 account

	£		£
Opening WIP	55,160	Transfer to finished	
Transfer from process 2	394,200	goods stock	581,888
Materials	110,520	Abnormal loss	192
Conversion costs	76,506	Closing WIP	54,306
	636,386		636,386

(b) Normal losses are unavoidable losses that are expected to occur under efficient operating conditions. They are an expected production cost and should
be absorbed by the completed production whereas abnormal losses are not
included in the process costs but are removed from the appropriate process
account and reported separately as an abnormal loss. See the section on
equivalent production and normal losses in Chapter 6 for a more detailed
explanation of the treatment of normal losses.

(c) If the weighted average method is used, both the units and value of WIP are
merged with current period costs and production to calculate the average cost
per unit. The weighted average cost per unit is then applied to all completed
units, any abnormal losses and closing WIP equivalent units. In contrast, with
the FIFO method the opening WIP is assumed to be the first group of units
completed during the current period. The opening WIP is charged separately
to completed production, and the cost per unit is based only on current costs
and production for the period. The closing WIP is assumed to come from the
new units that have been started during the period.

Answer to question 6.23

(a) It is assumed that the normal loss occurs at the start of the process and should
be allocated to completed production and closing WIP. It is also assumed that
process 2 conversion costs are not incurred when losses occur. Therefore
losses should not be allocated to conversion costs.

Statement of input and output (units):

	Input		Output
Opening WIP	1,200	Completed output	105,400
Transferred from		WIP	1,600
Process 1	112,000	Normal loss	
		(5% × 112,000)	5,600
		Abnormal loss (balance)	600
	113,200		113,200

Since the loss occurs at the start of the process it should be allocated over all
units that have reached this point. Thus the normal loss should be allocated to
all units of output. This can be achieved by adopting the short-cut method
described in Chapter 6 whereby the normal loss is not included in the unit
cost statement.

Calculation of cost per unit and cost of completed production (FIFO method):

	Current costs £	Completed units less opening WIP equiv. units	Abnormal loss	Closing WIP equiv. units	Current total equiv. units	Cost per unit £
Previous process cost	187,704					
Materials	47,972					
	235,676	104,200(105,400 − 1200)	600	1,600	106,400	2.215
Conversion costs	63,176	104,800(105,400 − 600)	–	1,200	106,000	0.596
	298,852					2.811

Cost of completed production:	£	£
Opening WIP (given)	3,009	
Previous process cost and materials (104,200 × £2.215)	230,803	
Conversion cost (104,800 × £0.596)	62,461	296,273
Abnormal Loss (600 × £2.215)		1,329
Closing WIP:		
Previous process cost and materials (1,600 × £2.215)	3,544	
Conversion costs (1,200 × £0.596)	715	4,259
		301,861

Process 2 account

	£		£
Opening WIP	3,009	Transfer to finished goods	296,273
Transfers from Process 1	187,704	Abnormal loss	1,329
Raw materials	47,972	Closing WIP	4 259
Conversion costs	63,176		
	301,861		301,861

(b) If the loss occurs at the end of the process then the normal loss should only be charged to those units that have reached the end of the process. In other words, the cost of normal losses should not be allocated to closing WIP. To meet this requirement a separate column for normal losses is incorporated into the unit cost statement and the normal loss equivalent units are included in the calculation of total equivalent units. The cost of the normal loss should be calculated and added to the cost of completed production. For an illustration of the approach see the section on equivalent production and normal losses in Chapter 6.

Joint product and by-product costing

Answers to Chapter 7

Question summary

7.1
Multiple choice questions.

7.2 to 7.4
Discussion problems on joint and by-products.

7.5 to 7.7
Preparation of process accounts and the apportionment of joint costs to products. Question 7.6 is also concerned with the accounting treatment of by-products and 7.7 requires a decision on further processing.

7.8
Preparation of a flow chart for joint and by-products and calculation of a cost per unit.

7.9 to 7.16
Apportionment of joint costs and decisions on whether or not a product should be further processed. Question 7.9 also requires the preparation of the process accounts and the accounting entries for joint and by-products.

Answer to question 7.1

	£
Joint costs apportioned to P (4,500/9,750 × £117,000) =	54,000
Further processing costs (4,500 × £9) =	40,500
Total cost	94,500
Sales revenues (4,050 × £25)	101,250
Profit	6,750

Answer = A

Answer to question 7.5

(a)   *Process 1 account*

	kg	£		kg	£
Materials	7,000	3,500	Normal loss (W2)	700	280
Labour and overhead		4,340	Transferred to		
Abnormal gain (W3)	130	156	process 2 (W1)	6,430	7,716
	7,130	7,996		7,130	7,996

Workings:

(W1)

$$\text{Cost per unit} = \frac{\text{Cost of production (£7,840)} - \text{Scrap value of normal loss (£280)}}{\text{Expected output (6,300 kg)}}$$

$$= £1.20 \text{ per kg}$$

(W2) Normal loss is 10% of *total* output, which in this case is equivalent to total input [therefore normal loss = $(10\% \times (6,430 + 570))$].

(W3) Abnormal gain = Actual output (6,430) − Expected output (6,300)

Normal loss account					Abnormal gain account		
	£		£		£		
Process 1		Abnormal		Normal loss		Process 1	156
(700 × 40p)	280	gain a/c		(130 × 40p)	52		
		(130 × 40p)	52	P & L a/c	104		
		Cash					
		(570 × 40p)	228				
	280		280		156		156

Process 2 account:

	kg	£		kg	£
Previous process			By-product net		
cost	6,430	7,716	income	430	645
Labour and			Output to be		
overhead		12,129	account for		19,200
			E	2,000	
			F	4,000	
	6,430	19,845		6,430	19,845

(b) The allocation of £19,200 to E and F depends on the apportionment method used.

  (i) *Physical output method:*

	E	F
	£	£
1. Total output cost	$6,400 \left(\dfrac{2,000}{6,000} \times £19,200 \right)$	$12,800 \left(\dfrac{4,000}{6,000} \times £19,200 \right)$
2. Closing stock	$2,880 \left(\dfrac{2,000 - 1,100}{2,000} \times £6,400 \right)$	$2,560 \left(\dfrac{4,000 - 3,200}{4,000} \times £12,800 \right)$

3. Cost of sales $3,520 \left(\dfrac{1,100}{2,000} \times £6,400 \right)$ $\qquad$ $10,240 \left(\dfrac{3,200}{4,000} \times £12,800 \right)$

4. Sales revenue $7,700 \ (1,100 \times £7)$ $\qquad$ $8,000 \ (3,200 \times £2.50)$

5. Profit $(4-3)$ $\quad$ 4,180 $\qquad$ (2,240)

(ii) *Market value of output method:*

	E	F
	£	£

1. Market value output $\quad 14,000 \ (2,000 \times £7)$ $\qquad 10,000 \ (4,000 \times £2.50)$

2. Cost of output $\quad 11,200 \left(\dfrac{14}{24} \times £19,200 \right)$ $\qquad 8,000 \left(\dfrac{10}{24} \times £19,200 \right)$

3. Closing stock $\quad 5,040 \left(\dfrac{900}{2,000} \times £11,200 \right)$ $\qquad 1,600 \left(\dfrac{800}{4,000} \times £8,000 \right)$

4. Cost of sales $\quad 6,160 \left(\dfrac{1,100}{2,000} \times £11,200 \right)$ $\qquad 6,400 \left(\dfrac{3,200}{4,000} \times £8,000 \right)$

5. Sales revenue $\quad 7,700$ $\qquad 8,000$

6. Profit $(5-4)$ $\quad 1,540$ $\qquad 1,600$

(c) See Chapter 7 for the answer to this question. In particular, the answer should stress that joint cost apportionments are necessary for stock valuation, but such apportionments are inappropriate for decision-making. For decision-making relevant costs should be used. It can be seen from the answer to part (b) that one method of apportionment implies that F makes a loss whereas the other indicates that F makes a profit. Product F should only be deleted if the costs saved from deleting it exceed the revenues lost.

Answer to question 7.7

(a) Normal loss (toxic waste) = 50 kg per 1,000 kg of input (i.e. 5%)
Actual input = 10,000 kg
Abnormal loss = Actual toxic waste (600) less normal loss (500) = 100 kg

By-product R net revenues of £1,750 are credited to the joint (main) process account and normal and abnormal losses are valued at the average cost per unit of output:

$$\frac{\text{Net cost of production } (£35,750 - £1,750)}{\text{Expected output of the joint products } (8,500 \text{ kg})} = £4$$

The cost of the output of the joint products is £33,600 (8,400 kg × £4) and this is to be allocated to the individual products on the basis of final sales value (i.e. 4,800 kg × £5 = £24,000 for P and 3,600 kg × £7 = £25,200 for Q):

P = £24,000/£49,200 × £33,600 = £16,390
Q = £25,200/£49,200 × £33,600 = £17,210

The main process account is as follows:

Main process account

	kg	£		kg	£
Materials	10,000	15,000	P Finished goods	4,800	16,390
Direct labour	–	10,000	Q Process 2	3,600	17,210
Variable overhead	–	4,000	By-product R	1,000	1,750
Fixed overhead	–	6,000	Normal toxic waste	500	–
Toxic waste disposal a/c	–	750	Abnormal toxic waste	100	400
	10,000	35,750		10,000	35,750

(b)

Toxic waste disposal (Creditors' Account)

	£		£
Bank	900	Main process account	750
		Abnormal toxic waste	150
	900		900

Abnormal toxic waste account

	£		£
Main process account	400	Profit and Loss Account	550
Toxic waste disposal account	150		
$(100 \times £1.50)$			
	550		550

Process 2 account

	kg	£		kg	£
Main process Q	3,600	17,210	Finished goods Q[b]	3,300	26,465
Fixed cost		6,000	Closing work-in-progress[b]	300	1,920
Variable cost		5,175[a]			
	3,600	28,385		3,600	28,385

Notes:
[a] $3,300 + (50\% \times 300) \times £1.50 = £5,175$
[b]

	£	Completed units	WIP equiv. units	Total equiv. units	Cost per unit
Previous process cost	17,210	3,300	300	3,600	4.78
Conversion cost	11,175	3,300	150	3,450	3.24
					8.02

	£
Completed units (3,300 units $\times$ £8.02)	26,465
WIP (300 $\times$ £4.78) + (150 $\times$ £3.24)	1,920
	28,385

(c)   See the section on methods of apportioning joint costs to joint products in Chapter 7 for the answer to this question.

(d)

	£
Incremental sales revenue per kg from further processing (£7 − £4.30)	2.70
Incremental (variable) cost per kg of further processing	1.50
Incremental contribution per kg from further processing	1.20

	£
At an output of 3,600 kg the incremental contribution is	4,320
Avoidable fixed costs	3,600
Net benefit	720

$$\text{Break-even point} = \frac{\text{Avoidable fixed costs (£3,600)}}{\text{Incremental unit contribution (£1.20)}} = 3,000 \text{ kg}$$

Further processing should be undertaken if output is expected to exceed 3,000 kg per week.

Answer to question 7.8

(a) See Figure Q7.7.

Workings:
(W1) (4,000 + 2,600 − 300)/900 = £7
(W2) (2,100 + 3,300)/300 = £18

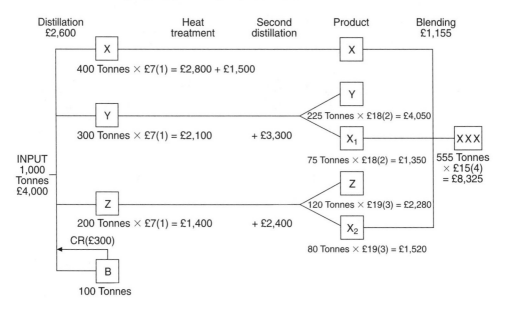

Figure Q7.7

(W3) (1,400 + 2,400)/200 = £19
(W4) (2,800 + 1,500 + 1,155 + 1,350 + 1,520)/555 = £15

Product	Output (tonnes)	Total cost £	Cost per tonne £
XXX	555	8,325	15
Y	225	4,050	18
Z	120	2,280	19

(c) An alternative treatment is to credit the income direct to the profit and loss account rather than crediting the proceeds to the process from which the by-product was derived.

Answer to question 7.10

(a)

	B £	K £	C £	Total £
Revenue	35,000	50,000	60,000	
Pre-separation joint costs (1)	17,500	12,500	10,000	
Post separation costs	20,000	10,000	22,500	
Profit/(loss)	(2,500)	27,500	27,500	52,500

(b)

	B	K	C	
Incremental costs	20,000	10,000	22,500	
Incremental revenue	14,000	30,000	42,000	
Incremental benefit	(6,000)	20,000	19,500	

Therefore profit will increase by £6,000 if B is sold at split-off point and the revised profit statements will be:

Revenue	21,000	50,000	60,000	
Pre-separation costs[a]	17,500	12,500	10,000	
Post separation costs	–	10,000	22,500	
Profit	3,500	27,500	27,500	58,500

Note:
[a] $B = 3,500/8,000 \times £40,000$; $K = 2,500/8,000 \times £40,000$; $C = 2,000/8,000 \times £40,000$.

Answer to question 7.12

(a) (i)

Product	(1) Sales value of production £	(2) Proportion to total	(3) Joint costs apportioned (1) £	(4) Cost per kg (2) £	(5) Stock valuation (3) £
A	700,000	7/30	420,000	30	60,000
B	1,200,000	4/10	720,000	36	108,000
C	1,000,000	1/3	600,000	24	96,000
D	100,000	1/30	60,000	60	60,000
	3,000,000		1,800,000		324,000

(1) Column 2 × £1,800,000.
(2) Joint cost apportioned ÷ kg produced.
(3) (Sales − production) × cost per kg.

(ii)

		£	£
Sales:	A (12.000 × £50) =	600,000	
	B (17,000 × £60) =	1,020,000	
	C (21000 × £40) =	840,000	2,460,000
Joint cost of production		1,800,000	
Less closing stock		324,000	1,476,000
Profit			984,000

(b) Cost information for decision-making should not be based on joint cost allocations and yet the question is requiring candidates to use joint cost allocations. The correct approach is to compare additional relevant revenues with additional relevant costs:

	A £	B £	C £
Additional revenues	10	10	10
Additional variable cost	7	8	9
Contribution to fixed costs	3	2	1
Additional fixed costs per month (Cost ÷ 72 months)	20,000	16,000	12,000
Number of units sold to justify further processing (Fixed costs ÷ Unit contribution)	6,667	8,000	12,000

As long as the average monthly sales exceed the above output levels further processing is justified.

An alternative approach would be:

	A £	B £	C £	Total
Additional sales revenue per month	120,000	170.000	210,000	
Additional variable costs per month	(84,000)	(136,000)	(189,000)	
Additional depreciation per month	(20,000)	(16,000)	(12,000)	
Additional monthly profit	16,000	18,000	9,000	43,000

The above calculations are based on the sales volume given in part (a) of the question.

Answer to question 7.15

(a) You can see from the question that the input is 240,000 kg and the output is 190,000 kg. It is assumed that the difference of 50,000 kg is a normal loss in output which occurs at the start of processing. Therefore the loss should be charged to the completed production and WIP. By making no entry for normal losses in the cost per unit calculation the normal loss is automatically apportioned between completed units and WIP.

	Opening WIP £	Current cost £	Total cost £	Completed units	Closing WIP	Total equivalent units	Cost per unit £	WIP value £
Materials	20,000	75,000	95,000	160,000	30,000	190,000	0.50	15,000
Processing costs	12,000	96,000	108,000	160,000	20,000	180,000	0.60	12,000
			203,000				1.10	27,000
			Completed units (160,000 units × £1.10)					176,000
								203,000

(b) This question requires a comparison of incremental revenues and incremental costs. Note that the costs of process 1 are irrelevant to the decision since they will remain the same whichever of the two alternatives are selected. You should also note that further processing 120,000 kg of the compound results in 240,000 kg of Starcomp.

Incremental sales revenue:

	£	£
Starcomp (120,000 × 2 kg × £2)	480,000	
Compound (120,000 × £1.60)	192,000	288,000
Incremental costs:		
Materials	120,000	
Processing costs	120,000	240,000
Incremental profits		48,000

It is therefore worthwhile further processing the compound.

(c) The sales revenue should cover the additional costs of further processing the 40,000 kg compound and the lost sales revenue from the 40,000 kg compound if it is sold without further processing.
  Additional processing costs:

	£
Materials (£160,000 − £120,000)	40,000
Processing costs (£140,000 − £120,000)	20,000
Lost compound sales revenue (40,000 × £1.60)	64,000
	124,000

$$\text{Minimum selling price per kg of Starcomp} = \frac{£124,000}{40,000 \text{ kg} \times 2}$$

$$= £1.55$$

Answer to question 7.16

(a) *Profit and loss account:*

	W £	X £	Z £	Total £
Opening stock	–	–	8,640	8,640
Production cost	189,060	228,790	108,750	526,600
Less closing stock	(14,385)	(15,070)	(15,010)	(44 465)
Cost of sales	174,675	213,720	102,380	490,775
Selling and administration costs	24,098	97,768	10,011	61,877
Total costs	198,773	241,488	112,391	552,652
Sales	240,975	277,680	100,110	618,765
Profit/(loss)	42,202	36,192	(12,281)	66,113

Workings:
Joint process cost per kilo of output = £0.685 per kg (£509,640/744,000 kg)
Production cost for products W, X and Y:

Product W (276,000 kg × £0.685) = £189,060
  X (334,000 kg × £0.685) = £228,790
  Y (134,000 kg × £0.685) = £91,790

Closing stocks for products W and X:

Product W (21,000 kg × £0.685) = £14,385
  X (22,000 kg × £0.685) = £15,070

Cost per kilo of product Z:

	£
Product Y (128,000 kg × £0.685) =	87,680
Further processing costs	17,920
Less by-product sales (8,000 × £0.12) =	(960)
	104,640

Cost per kilo (£104,640/96,000 kg) £1.09

Closing stock of product Z (10,000 kg × £1.09)   =   £10,900
Add closing stock of input Y (6,000 × £0.685)   =   £4,110

Closing stock relating to product Z   £15,010

Production cost relating to final product Z:

	£
Product Y (134,000 kg × £0.685) =	91,790
Further processing costs	17,920
Less by-product costs	(960)
	108,750

(b)   The joint costs are common and unavoidable to both alternatives, and are therefore not relevant for the decision under consideration. Further processing from an input of 128,000 kg of Y has resulted in an output of 96,000 kg of Z. Thus it requires 1.33 kg of Y to produce 1 kg of Z (128/96).

	£
Revenue per kilo for product Z	1.065 (£100,110/94,000 kg)
Sale proceeds at split-off point	
(1.33 × £0.62)	0.823
Incremental revenue per kg from further	
processing	0.242
Incremental costs of further processing	0.177 [(£17,920 − £960)/96,000]
Incremental profit from further processing	0.065

It is assumed that selling and administration costs are fixed and will be unaffected by which alternative is selected. The company should therefore process Y further into product Z and not accept the offer from the other company to purchase the entire output of product Y.

(c)   See the section on methods of apportioning joint costs to joint products in Chapter 7 for the answer to this question.

Absorption costing and variable costing

Answers to Chapter 8

Question summary

8.1 and 8.2
Multiple choice questions.

8.3 and 8.4
Discussion questions relating to Chapter 8.

8.5 to 8.15
Preparation of variable costing and absorption costing profit statements and computation of stock valuations. Questions 8.7, 8.9, 811, 8.13 and 8.14 require the reconciliation of absorption costing and variable costing profits. Question 8.12 also requires a statement of equivalent production in order to calculate product costs. The most difficult questions are 8.13 to 8.15. Question 8.15 involves the reapportionment of service department costs and the calculation of overhead rates prior to the preparation of profit statements. Question 8.14 requires the preparation of absorption and variable costing statements using both FIFO and average costing methods.

Answer to question 8.1

Fixed overhead = £2 per unit (£60,000/30,000 units)
Because production exceeded sales by 180 units a sum of £360 (180 × £2) is included in the stock valuation and not charged as an expense of the current period. Fixed overheads of £4,640 (£5,000 monthly cost − £360) are therefore charged as an expense for the period.

	£
Contribution (2,220 units sales × £5.50)	12,210
Fixed overheads charged as an expense	4,640
Profit	7,570

Answer = B

Answer to question 8.2

Closing stock = 2,500 units (17,500 − 15,000)
With absorption costing fixed overheads of £10,000 (£2,500 units × £4) are deferred as a future expense whereas marginal costing treats fixed overheads as a period expense. Therefore absorption costing will be £10,000 greater.

Answer = B

Answer to question 8.6

(a) *Calculation of unit costs:*

Direct material cost	10.00
Direct wages cost	4.00
Variable overhead cost	2.50
Variable manufacturing cost	16.50
Fixed manufacturing overhead (£400,000/320,000 units)	1.25
Total manufacturing cost	17.75

Profit statements:

(i) Marginal costing	January–March £000	April–June £000
Opening stock	Nil	165
Production costs: variable	1,155 (70,000 × £16.50)	1,650 (100,000 × £16.50)
Closing stock	(165) (10,000 × £16.50)	(330) (20,000 × £16.50)
	990	1,485
Selling and distribution costs: variable	90	135
	1,080	1,620
Revenue from sales	2,700	4,050
Contribution	1,620	2,430
Fixed production costs	(100)	(100)
Fixed selling and distribution costs	(20)	(20)
Fixed administration costs	(30)	(30)
Budgeted profit	1,470	2,280

(ii) Absorption costing	£000	£000
Opening stock	Nil	177.5
Total production costs	1,242.5 (70,000 × £17.75)	1,775.0 (100,000 × £17.75)
	1,242.5	1 952.5
Closing stock	(177.5) (10,000 × £17.75)	(355.0) (20,000 × £17.75)
	1,065.0	1,597.5

Add under-absorption of production overhead (10,000 × 1.25)	12.5	–
Loss over-absorption of production overhead (20,000 × 1.25)	–	(25.0)
Total selling and distribution costs	110.0	155.0
Administration costs	30.0	30.0
	1,217.5	1,757.5
Revenue from sales	2,700.0	4,050.0
Budgeted profit	1,482.5	2,292.5

(b) The difference in profits of £12,500 is due to the fact that part of the fixed production overheads (10,000 units at £1.25 per unit) are included in the closing stock valuation and not recorded as an expense during the current period. With the marginal costing system all of the fixed manufacturing costs incurred during a period are recorded as an expense of the current period.

(c) It is assumed that the question requires the production overhead account to be written up only in respect of fixed production overhead.

Fixed production overhead control account:

	£		£
Actual expenditure	102,400	WIP a/c (74,000 × £1.25)	92,500
		Under-absorption transferred to P & L a/c	9,900
	102,400		102,400

(d) See the section on some arguments in support of variable costing in Chapter 8 for the answer to this question.

Answer to question 8.9

(a) Variable cost per unit:

	£
Variable production cost	49
Variable non-manufacturing costs (20% off sales value)	28
	77
Manufacturing absorption cost per unit	69

Fixed costs for the period (£20 × 16,000 units) £320,000 per annum
(£160,000 per six months)

(i) *Marginal costing profit statements:*

	March 1993 £		September 1993 £	
Opening stock			73,500	(1,500 × £49)
Variable production costs	416,500	(8,500 × £49)	343,000	(7,000 × £49)
Less closing stock	(73,500)	(1,500 × £49)	(24,500)	(500 × £49)
	343,000		392,000	
Variable non-manufacturing costs	196,000	(7,000 × £28)	224,000	(8,000 × £28)
	539,000		616,000	
Sales	980,000	(7,000 × £140)	1,120,000	(8,000 × £140)
Contribution	441,000		504,000	
Fixed costs				
(£160,000 + £180,000/2)	250,000		250,000	
Profit	191,000		254,000	

(ii) *Absorption costing profit statements:*

	March 1993 £		September 1993 £	
Opening stock	–		103,500	(1,500 × £69)
Production cost	586,500	(8,500 × £69)	483,000	(7,000 × £69)
Less closing stock	(103,500)	(1,500 × £69)	(34,500)	(500 × £69)
	483,000		552,000	
Under-/(over-)recovery fixed overheads	(10,000)	(500 × £20)	20,000	(1,000 × £20)
	473,000		572,000	
Variable non-manufacturing costs	196,000	(7,000 × £28)	224,000	(8,000 × £28)
Fixed non-manufacturing costs	90,000		90,000	
	759,000		886,000	
Sales	980,000		1,120,000	
Profit	221,000		234,000	

(b) With a marginal costing system all of the fixed manufacturing overhead incurred during a period is charged as an expense whereas fixed overheads are included in the stock valuations with the absorption costing system. In the first period fixed overheads of £30,000 (1,500 × £20) are included in the closing stock valuation and not charged as an expense of the current period. Therefore the absorption costing profits exceed the marginal costing profits by £30,000. In the second period stocks increase by 1,000 units and the absorption costing statement includes £20,000 (1,000 × £20) in the stock movements. This results in absorption costing profits being £20,000 less than the marginal costing profits. The following is a reconciliation of the profit statements:

	31st March £	30th September £
Marginal costing profits	191,000	254,000
Fixed production overheads included in increases/(decreases) in stock movements	30,000	(20,000)
	221,000	234,000

(c) For an explanation of those situations where marginal costing may be beneficial in making decisions you should refer to Chapter 10 in respect of the following situations:
  (i) deleting a segment;
  (ii) make-or-buy decisions;
  (iii) pricing decisions;
  (iv) product mix decisions where limiting factors exist.

Answer to question 8.11

(a) See sections on some arguments in support of variable costing and some
arguments in support of absorption costing in Chapter 8 for the answer to this
question.

(b) (i)

	£
Fixed production overhead per unit =	0.60 (£144,000/240,000 units)
Variable production cost per unit =	1.30 (£312,000/240,000 units)
Variable selling and administration overhead per unit =	0.10 (£24,000/240,000 units)
Fixed selling and administration overhead per unit =	0.40 (£96,000/240,000 units)
	2.40
Selling price	3.00
Profit	0.60

	£
Fixed production overhead incurred	144,000
Fixed production overhead absorbed (260,000 × £0.60)	156,000
Over-recovery	£12,000

(ii) *Absorption costing profit:*

	£
Opening stock (40,000 × £1.90)	76,000
Production cost (260,000 × £1.90)	494,000
	570,000
Less closing stock (70,000 × £1.90)	133,000
Cost of sales (230,000 × £1.90)	437,000
Less over recovery of fixed production overhead	12,000
	425,000
Selling and administration overhead:	
Variable (230,000 × £0.10)	23,000
Fixed	96,000
Total cost	544,000
Sales (230,000 × £3)	690,000
Profit	£146,000

Marginal costing profit:

	£
Contribution (230,000 × (£3 − £1.40))	368,000
Less fixed costs (£144 000 + £96,000)	240,000
Profit	£128,000

(iii)

	£
Absorption costing profit	146,000
Fixed overhead included in stock increase (30,000 × £0.60)	18,000
Marginal costing profit	£128,000

(iv) The profit figure will be the same with both systems whenever production equals sales and therefore opening stock equals closing stock.

Answer to question 8.12

(a)

Cost element	Total cost £	Completed units	WIP equivalent units	Total equivalent units	Cost per unit £	WIP £
Materials	714,000	98,000	4,000	102,000	7.00	28,000
Labour	400,000	98,000	2,000	100,000	4.00	8,000
Variable overhead	100,000	98,000	2,000	100,000	1.00	2,000
Fixed overhead	350,000	98,000	2,000	100,000	3.50	7,000
	1,564,000				15.50	45,000

(b) *Absorption costing profit statement:*

	£	£
Sales		1,800,000
Production cost	1,564,000	
Closing WIP	(45,000)	
Closing finished goods stock (8,000 × £15.50)	(124,000)	1,395,000
Gross profit		405,000
Less: Variable selling and administration		
costs (£1.60 × 90,000)		(144,000)
Fixed selling and administration costs		(250,000)
Net profit		£11,000

(c) *Marginal costing profit statement:*

	£	£
Sales		1,800,000
Variable cost of production	1,214,000	
Closing WIP	(38,000)	
Closing finished goods stock (8,000 × £12)	(96,000)	
Variable cost of sales	1,080,000	
Variable selling and administration costs	144,000	1,224,000
Contribution		576,000
Less: Fixed costs (350 + 200 + 50)		(600,000)
Net loss		£(24,000)

(d) The absorption costing statement shows a profit of £11,000 whereas the marginal costing statement shows a net loss of £24,000. The difference of £35,000 is due to the fact that the closing stock valuation includes £35,000 fixed overhead (£7,000 WIP and £28,000 finished goods) whereas the fixed overheads are not included in the stock valuation when the marginal costing approach is used. Instead, all the fixed overheads are charged as a period cost. With the absorption costing system, the fixed overheads of £35,000 that are included in the stock valuation will be recorded as an expense when the stocks are sold. Consequently, the absorption costing method shows £35,000 greater profits than the marginal costing method. For a detailed discussion of a comparison of the impact on profits of the two methods see Chapter 8.

For internal profit measurement purposes both methods are acceptable, but for external reporting SSAP 9 requires that stocks should be valued on an absorption costing basis.

Answer to question 8.13

(a)
$$\text{Break-even point} = \frac{\text{Fixed costs (£180,000)}}{\text{Unit contribution (£10 − £6)}} = 45,000 \text{ units per period}$$

(b)

	Period 1 £000	Period 2 £000	Period 3 £000
Opening stock	–	180	–
Production cost at £9 per unit (*W1*)	630 (70 × £9)	360 (40 × £9)	540 (60 × £9)
	630	540	540
Less closing stock	180 (20 × £9)	–	180 (20 × £9)
	450	540	360
Under-/(over-)recovery of fixed overheads (*W2*)	(30)	60	–
Variable overhead expenditure variance (*W3*)	(2)	5	–
Total cost	418	605	360
Sales	500	600	400
Profit/(loss)	82	(5)	40

Workings:

		£	
(W1)	Variable cost per unit	6	
	Fixed costs per unit	3	(£180,000/60,000 units)
		9	

(W2) Period 1 10,000 units at £3
       2 20,000 units at £3
       3 Actual production = normal activity

(W3) Actual variable cost is compared with budgeted variable costs for actual production, and the difference represents under/over spending

Period 1 $(70,000 \times £1) - £68,000 = £2,000$ Favourable variance
        2 $(40,000 \times £1) - £45,000 = £5,000$ Adverse variance
        3 $(60,000 \times £1) - £60,000 = 0$

(c)

	Period 1 £000	Period 2 £000	Period 3 £000
Contribution from output differing from break-even point (W1)	+20	+60	−20
Fixed overhead included in stock changes (W2)	+60	−60	+60
Variable overhead expenditure variance	+2	−5	0
Profit for period	82	−5	+40

Workings:

(W1)	$(50 - 45) \times £4$	$(60 - 45) \times £4$	$(40 - 45) \times £4$
(W2)	$(+20 \times £3)$	$(-20 \times £3)$	$(+20 \times £3)$

In period 1 sales volume was 5,000 units in excess of the break-even sales volume, and at a contribution of £5 per unit a profit of £20,000 would result if calculated on a marginal costing basis. However, actual profit was £82,000. There are two reasons for this. First, absorption costing has been used and £60,000 (20,000 units × £3) fixed overheads has been carried forward in fixed overheads and thus deferred as an expense. The break-even point calculation assumes a marginal costing system with fixed overheads of £180,000 per period being regarded as a period cost. Secondly, the break-even analysis and stock valuations assume variable overheads will be £1 per unit of output. In period 1 output was 70,000 units and expected variable overhead expenditure was £70,000. Actual expenditure was £68,000, thus resulting in an increase in profits of £2,000

Similar comments apply to periods 2 and 3, but note that the opening stock exceeds closing stock by 20,000 units in period 2. Consequently, £60,000 fixed overheads (20,000 units × £3) are included as an expense in the opening stock, but since closing stock is zero no fixed overheads are deferred as an expense until period 3. Therefore the total fixed overhead charged for period 2 is £240,000 (£180,000 + £60,000 included in the opening stock).

Answer to question 8.14

(a) $\text{Fixed overhead rate per unit} = \dfrac{\text{Budgeted fixed overheads (£300,000)}}{\text{Budgeted production (40,000 units)}} = £7.50$

Absorption Costing (FIFO) Profit Statement:

		£000
Sales (42,000 × £72)		3,024
Less cost of sales:		
Opening stock (2,000 × £30)	60	
Add production (46,000 × £52,50[a])	2,415	
	2,475	
Less closing stock (6,000 × £52.50)	315	2,160
		864
Add over-absorption of overheads[b]		27
Profit		891

Notes:

[a] Variable cost per unit = £2,070/46,000 = £45
Total cost per unit = £45 + £7.50 Fixed overhead = £52.50
[b] Overhead absorbed (46,000 × £7.50) = £345,000
Actual overhead incurred = £318,000
Over-recovery = £27,000

Marginal Costing (FIFO) Profit Statement:

	£000	£000
Sales		3,024
Less Cost of Sales:		
Opening stock (2,000 × £25)	50	
Add Production (46,000 × £45)	2,070	
	2,120	
Less closing stock (6,000 × £45)	270	1,850
Contribution		1,174
Less fixed overheads incurred		318
Profit		856

Reconciliation:

Absorption profit exceeds marginal costing profit by £35,000 (£891,000 − £856,000). The difference is due to the fixed overheads carried forward in the stock valuations:

	£
Fixed overheads in closing stocks (6,000 × £7.50)	45,000
Less fixed overheads in opening stocks (2,000 × £5)	10,000
Fixed overheads included in stock movement	35,000

Absorption costing gives a higher profit because more of the fixed overheads are carried forward into the next accounting period than were brought forward from the last accounting period.

(b) *Absorption costing (AVECO) Profit Statement:*

	£000	£000
Sales		3,024
Opening stock plus production		
(48,000 × £51.56[a])	2,475	
Less closing stock (6,000 × £51.56)	309	2,166
		858
Add over-absorption of overheads		27
Profit		885

Marginal Costing (AVECO) Profit Statement:

	£000	£000
Sales		3,024
Less cost of sales		
Opening stock plus production		
(48,000 × £44.17[b])	2,120	
Less closing stock (6,000 × £44.17)	265	1,855
Contribution		1,169
Less fixed overheads		318
Profit		851

Notes:
[a] With the AVECO method the opening stock is merged with the production of the current period to ascertain the average unit cost:
Opening stock (2,000 × £30) + Production cost (£2,415,000) = £2,475,000
Average cost per unit = £2,475,000/48,000 units
[b] Average cost = (Production cost (£2,070,000)
+ Opening stock (50,000))/48,000 units.

Reconciliation:

	£000s
Difference in profits (£885 − £851)	34
Fixed overheads in closing stocks (309 − 265)	44
Less fixed overheads in opening stock (2,000 × £5)	10
Fixed overheads included in stock movement	34

The variations in profits between (a) and (b) are £6,000 for absorption costing and £5,000 for marginal costing. With the FIFO method all of the lower cost brought forward from the previous period is charged as an expense against the current period. The closing stock is derived only from current period costs. With the AVECO method the opening stock is merged with the units produced in the current period and is thus allocated between cost of sales and closing stocks, Therefore some of the lower cost brought forward from the previous period is incorporated in the closing stock at the end of the period.

Cost–volume–profit analysis

Answers to Chapter 9

Question summary

9.1 to 9.7
Multiple choice questions.

9.8 to 9.10
Discussion question on cost–volume–profit (CVP) analysis.

9.11 to 9.17
Construction of break-even or profit-volume graphs. Question 9.12 requires the calculation of variable costs using the high-low method of analysing fixed and variable costs. Question 9.15 includes a change in the sales mix and Question 9.16 requires the preparation of a multi-product profit–volume graph. Question 9.17 includes an increase in fixed costs.

9.18 to 9.24
These questions consist of a variety of CVP analysis problems using a non-graphical approach. Question 9.22 also requires the separation of fixed and variable costs using the high-low method.

9.25
A simple problem which can be used to illustrate the product mix assumptions of CVP analysis.

9.26 and 9.27
More difficult questions requiring the calculation of break-even points based on different sales mix assumptions. Question 9.27 also involves a product abandonment decision.

9.28 to 9.34
More demanding CVP analysis problems using a non-graphical approach. These problems place a greater emphasis on decision-making aspects. Question 9.30 also involves key factor decision-making.

Answer to question 9.1

	Product X	Product Y	Total
Budgeted sales volume (units)	80,000	20,000	
Budgeted contribution per unit	£4	£5	
Budgeted total contribution	£320,000	£100,000	£420,000
Budgeted sales revenue	£960,000	£160,000	£1,120,000

Average contribution per unit = £420,000/100,000 units = £4.20

$$\text{Break-even point} = \frac{\text{Fixed costs (£273,000)}}{\text{Average contribution per unit (£4.20)}} = 65,000 \text{ units}$$

Average selling price per unit = £1,120,000/100,000 units = £11.20

Break-even point in sales revenue = 65,000 units × £11.20 = £728,000

Answer = D

Answer to question 9.2

$$\text{Average contribution to sales ratio} = \frac{(40\% \times 1) + (50\% \times 3)}{4} = 47.5\%$$

Break-even point is at the point where 47.5% of the sales equal the fixed costs (i.e. £120,000/0.475 = £252,632).

$$\text{In other words, the break-even point} = \frac{\text{Fixed costs}}{\text{PV ratio}}$$

Answer = C

Answer to question 9.3

	Total cost (1,000 units) £	Total cost (2,000 units) £
Production overhead	3,500 (£3.50 × 1,000)	5,000 (£2.50 × 2,000)
Selling overhead	1,000 (£1 × 1,000)	1,000 (£0.5 × 2,000)

$$\text{Variable cost per unit} = \frac{\text{Change in cost}}{\text{Change in activity}}$$

Production overhead = £1,500/1,000 units = £1.50
Selling overhead = Fixed cost since total costs remain unchanged.
The unit costs of direct materials are constant at both activity levels and are therefore variable.
Production overheads fixed cost element = Total cost (£3,500) − Variable cost
(1,000 × £1.50) = £2,000
Total fixed cost = £2,000 + £1,000 = £3,000
Unit variable cost £4 + £3 + £1.50 = £8.50

Answer = E

Answer to question 9.4

Contribution/sales (%) = (0.33 × 40% Aye) + (0.33 × 50% Bee) + (0.33 × ? Cee)
= 48%
Cee = 54% (Balancing figure)
The total contribution/sales ratio for the revised sales mix is:
(0.40 × 40% Aye) + (0.25 × 50% Bee) + (0.35 × 54% Cee) = 47.4%

Answer = C

Answer to question 9.5

Sales	100	110 (100 + 10%)
Variable cost	60	60
Contribution	40	50
Increase = 25%		

Answer = D

Answer to question 9.6

Contribution per unit = 40% × £20 = £8

$$\text{Break-even point} = \frac{\text{Fixed costs (£60,000)}}{\text{Contribution per unit (£8)}} = 7,500 \text{ units}$$

Answer = E

Answer to question 9.7

Change in activity = 2,350 m^2
Change in costs = £9,635
Variable cost per metre = £4.10 (£9,635/2,350)
Fixed costs at 15,100 m^2 = £21,675 (£83,585 − (15,100 × £4.10))
Total cost at 16,200 m^2 = £88,095 (£21,675 + (16,200 × £4.10))

Answer = A

Answer to question 9.11

(a) See Figure Q9.11.
(b) See Chapter 9 for the answer to this question.
(c) The major limitations are:
    (i) Costs and revenue may only be linear within a certain output range.
    (ii) In practice, it is difficult to separate fixed and variable costs, and the calculations will represent an approximation.
    (iii) It is assumed that profits are calculated on a variable costing basis.

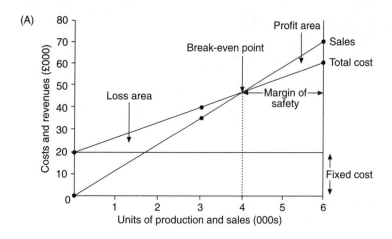

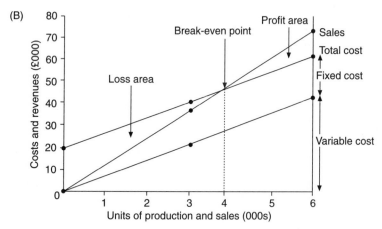

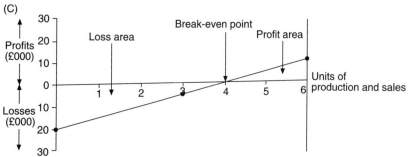

Figures Q9.11 *(A) Break-even chart. (B) Contribution graph. (C) Profit–volume graph.*

      (iv)   Analysis assumes a single product is sold or a constant sales mix is maintained.

  (d) The advantages are:

      (i)   The information can be absorbed at a glance without the need for detailed figures.

     (ii)   Essential features are emphasized.

   (iii)   The graphical presentation can be easily understood by non-accountants.

Answer to question 9.12

(a) This question requires the separation of total cost into the fixed and variable elements using the high-low method.

	Low £	High £
Sales at £30,000 per unit	480,000 (16 × £30 000	900,000 (30 × £30 000)
Profit	40,000	250,000
Total costs (difference)	440,000	650,000

An increase in output of 14 units results in an increase in total costs of £210,000. Assuming that fixed costs are constant for all activity levels the variable costs per unit is £15,000 (£210,000/14 units). At 30 units activity the variable costs will be £450,000 and monthly fixed costs are £200,000 (£650,000 − £450,000). Over a six-month period total fixed costs are £1,200,000.

Break-even point = Fixed costs (£1,200,000)/Unit contribution (£15,000)
= 80 units

See Figure Q9.12 for graph.

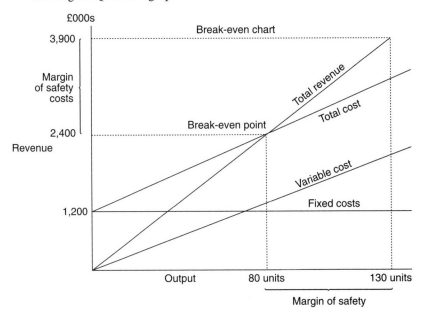

Figure Q9.12

(b) Revised unit contribution   £10,000
Revised total contribution   £143,000 (130 units × £1.10 × £10,000)
Revised profit   £230,000 (£1,430,000 − £1,200,000 fixed costs)
Revised profit   £750,000 (130 × £15,000 − £1,200,000 fixed costs)

The selling price should not be reduced because profits will decline by £520,000.

(c) Costs may not be variable and fixed throughout the entire production range. For example, unit variable cost may not be constant because of bulk discounts on purchases and increasing and decreasing returns (see the section on the economists' model, Chapter 9). Costs may also be semi-variable (see Chapter 2 for an explanation of these terms).

Answer to question 9.13

(a)

	August £	September £	Change £
Sales	80,000	90,000	10,000
Cost of sales	50,000	55,000	5,000
Selling and distribution	8,000	9,000	1,000
Administration	15,000	15,000	Nil

The only activity measure that is given is sales revenue. An increase in sales of £10,000 results in an increase in cost of sales of £5,000 and an increase in selling and distribution costs of £1,000. It is therefore assumed that the increase is attributable to variable costs and variable cost of sales is 50% of sales and variable selling and distribution costs are 10% of sales.

Fixed costs are derived by deducting variable costs from total costs for either month. The figures for August are used in the calculations below:

	Total cost £	Variable cost £	Fixed cost (Balance) £
Cost of sales	50,000	40,000	10,000
Selling and distribution	8,000	8,000	Nil
Administration	15,000	Nil	15,000
			25,000

Total cost = £25,000 fixed costs + variable costs (60% of sales)

(b) The following items are plotted on the graph:

	Variable cost	Total cost
Zero sales	Nil	£25,000 fixed cost
£80,000 sales	£48,000 (60%)	£73,000
£90,000 sales	£54,000 (60%)	£79,000
£50,000 sales	£30,000 (60%)	£55,000
£100,000 sales	£60,000	£85,000

$$\text{Break-even point} = \frac{\text{Fixed costs} (£25,000)}{\text{Contribution to sales ratio} (0.40)} = £62,500 \text{ sales}$$

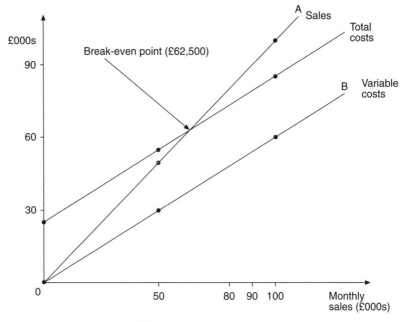

Area of contribution = Area AOB

Figure Q9.13 *Contribution break-even graph.*

(c)
		£
Actual sales = 1.3 × Break-even sales (£62,500)	=	81,250
Contribution (40% of sales)	=	32,500
Fixed costs	=	25,000
Monthly profit	=	7,500
Annual profit	=	90,000

(d)
		£
Annual contribution from single outlet (£32,500 × 12)	=	390,000
Contribution to cover lost sales (10%)	=	39,000
Specific fixed costs	=	100,000
Total contribution required		529,000

Required sales = £529,000/0.4 = £1,322,500

(e) The answer should draw attention to the need for establishing a sound system of budgeting and performance reporting for each of the different outlets working in close conjunction with central office. The budgets should be merged together to establish a master budget for the whole company.

Answer to question 9.15

(a)
$$\text{Break-even point} = \frac{\text{Fixed costs (£1,212,000)}}{\text{Average contribution per £ of sales (£0.505)}}$$

$$= £2,400,000$$

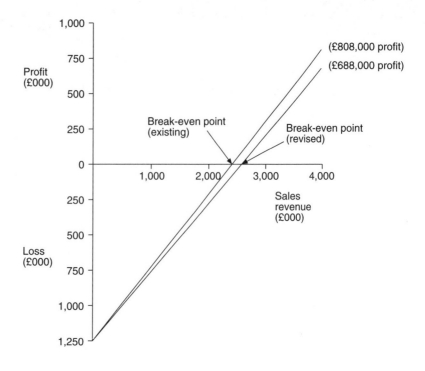

Figure Q9.15 *Profit–volume chart.*

Average contribution per £ of sales = $[0.7 \times (£1 - £0.45)] + [0.3 \times (£1 - £0.6)]$

(b) The graph (Figure Q9.15) is based on the following calculations:

Zero activity: loss = £1,212,000 (fixed costs)
£4 m existing sales: (£4 m × £0.505) − £1,212,000 = £808,000 profit
£4 m revised sales: (£4 m × £0.475) − £1,212,000 = £688,000 profit
Existing break-even point: £2,400,000
Revised break-even point: £2,551,579 (£1,212,000/£0.475)
Revised contribution per £ of sales: (0.5 × £0.55) + (0.5 × £0.40) = £0.475

(c) $\dfrac{\text{Required contribution}}{\text{Contribution per £ of sales}} = \dfrac{£455,000 + £700,000}{£0.55} = £2,100,000$

Answer to question 9.19

(a) BEP = Fixed cost (£210,000)/Contribution per unit (£17)
   = 12.353 units

Margin of safety:
Budgeted contribution   = £510,000 (£300,000 + £210,000)
Budgeted sales volume (units) = 30.000 (£510.000/£17)
Budgeted sales revenue   = £750,000 (30.000 × £25)
BEP (£)   = £308,825 (12,353 × £25)
Margin of safety   = £441,175

(b) Required total contribution   = £630,000 (£420,000 + £210,000)
    Required unit contribution   = £21 (£630,000/30,000 units)
    Required selling price   = £29 (£21 + £8 variable cost)
    Present selling price   = £25
    Required percentage increase = 16%

(c) *Proposal 1:*   £
    Total contribution   461,100 (31,800 × (£22.50 − £8))
    Fixed costs   210,000
    _____
    Profit   251,100
    _____

    Proposal 2:
    Total contribution   547,200 (28,800 × (£27 − £8))
    Fixed cost   210,000
    _____
    Profit   337,200
    _____

(d) For the answer to this question see section on the economists' model in Chapter 9. In particular, the answer should stress that revenue and cost functions may not be linear because:
   (i)   beyond a certain sales volume selling price may be reduced order to increase sales;
   (ii) quantity discounts may result in the material cost per unit changing for different output levels;
   (iii) at high output levels, bottlenecks may create inefficiences and cause increases in labour costs per unit of output;
   (iv) fixed costs may increase in step functions as new equipment is acquired to meet increased output.

Answer to question 9.21

(a) For a description of each of the items see:
   (i)   the section on normal and abnormal losses in Chapter 6.
   (ii) the section on performance reports in Chapter 15.
   (iii) the sections on control accounts and recording the issue of materials in Chapter 5.
   (iv) the section on under- and over-recovery of overheads in Chapter 4.

(b) (i) and (ii)

	£000s	£000s	£000s
Sales	600	700	800
Manufacturing costs	350	380	410

An increase in sales revenues of £100,000 results in an increase in total costs of £30,000. Variable costs are therefore 30% of sales. The cost structure is:

	£000s	£000s	£000s
Sales	600	700	800
Variable costs	180	210	240
Fixed costs (balance)	170	170	170
Total manufacturing costs	350	380	410

The contribution/sales ratios and total fixed costs for each alternative are:

	Agents	Sales force
Contribution/sales ratio	60%	70%
Fixed costs: Manufacturing (£000s)	170	170
Administration (£000s)	160	160
Selling (£000s)	–	60
Total	330	390

Note that the variable costs for the sales through agents alternative are 30% of sales (manufacturing) plus 10% of sales for commissions. Therefore the contribution/sales ratio is 60%.

Break-even point   =   Fixed costs/Contribution ratio
Sales through agents =   £330,000/0.6 = £550,000
Own sales force   =   £390,000/0.7 = £557,143

(b) (iii) Selling through own sales force has the higher break-even point because of the higher fixed costs. The statement shown below indicates that profits are identical for both alternatives at the lowest potential sales volume of £600,000. At higher levels of sales it is more profitable to employ the company's own sales force. This can be seen from the figures shown below. The company should therefore employ its own sales force.

Estimated profits for potential sales volumes:

(£000)	Low		Medium		High	
	Agent	Sales force	Agent	Sales force	Agent	Sales force
Sales	600	600	700	700	800	800
Contribution	360	420	420	490	480	560
Fixed costs	330	390	330	390	330	390
Net profit	30	30	90	100	150	170

Answer to question 9.23

(a) *With promotion:*

Unit variable cost	=	£1.54 (55% × £2.80)
Promotional selling price	=	£2.24 (80% × £2.80)
Promotional contribution per unit	=	£0.70
Contribution for 4 week promotion period	=	£16,800 (6,000 × 4 weeks × £0.70)
Less incremental fixed costs	=	£5,400
		£11,400

Without promotion:

Normal contribution per unit	=	£1.26 (£2.80 × 45%)
Contribution for 4 week period	=	£12,096 (£1.26 × 2,400 × 4 weeks)

Therefore the promotion results in a reduction in profits of £696.

(b) Required contribution = £17,496 (£12,096 + £5,400 fixed costs)
Required sales volume in units = 24,994 (£17,496/£0.70 unit contribution)
Required weekly sales volume = 6,249 units (24,994/4 weeks)
Sales multiplier required = 2.6 (6,249/2,400)

(c) Other factors to be considered are:
    (i) the effect of the promotion on sales after the promotion period;
    (ii) the impact of the promotion on sales of other products during and after the promotion.

Answer to question 9.24

(a) *Calculation of total contribution:*

		£
Product A (460,000 × £1.80)	=	828,000
Product B (1,000,000 × £0.78)	=	780,000
Product C (380,000 × £1.40)	=	532,000
		2,140,000

Calculation of total sales revenue:

		£
Product A (460,000 × £3)	=	1,380,000
Product B (1,000,000 × £2.45)	=	2,450,000
Product C (380,000 × £4)	=	1,520,000
		5,350,000

$$\text{Break-even point (sales revenue basis)} = \frac{\text{Fixed costs } (£1,710,000) \times (\text{total sales } (£5,350,000)}{\text{Total contribution } (2,140,000)}$$

$$= £4,275,000$$

(b) *£2.75 selling price:*

Total contribution 590,000 × (£2.75 − £1.20)	914,500
Existing planned contribution	828,000
Extra contribution	86,500
Less additional fixed costs	60,000
Additional contribution to general fixed costs	26,500

£2.55 selling price:

	£
Total contribution 650,000 × (£2.55 − £1.20)	877,500
Existing planned contribution	828,000
Extra contribution	49,500
Less additional fixed costs	60,000
Contribution to general fixed costs	(10,500)

It is worthwhile incurring the expenditure on advertising and sales promotion at a selling price of £2.75.

(c) Required contribution = Existing contribution (£828,000)
+ Additional fixed costs (£60,000)
= £888,000

The required sales volume at a selling price of £2.75 that will generate a total contribution of £888,000 is 572,903 units (£888,000/£1.55 unit contribution).

(d) See the section on margin of safety in Chapter 9 for the answer to this question. At the existing selling price for product A, the margin of safety for Z Ltd is £1,075,000 (£5,350,000 sales revenue − £4,275,000 break-even point) of sales revenue. This is 20.1% of the current level of sales. If Z Ltd incurs the advertising and promotion expenditure and reduces the selling price to £2.75 for product A, the break-even point will increase to £4,446,000 and total sales revenue will increase to £5,593,000 This will result in a margin of safety of £1,147,000 or 20.5% of sales.

Answer to question 9.25

$$\text{Break-even point} \quad \frac{\text{Fixed costs}}{\text{Contribution per unit}}$$

Product X	25,000 units (£100,000/£4)
Product Y	25,000 units (£200,000/£8)
Company as a whole	57,692 units (£300,000/£5.20^a)

Note:

$$^a \text{ Average contribution per unit} = \frac{(70,000 \times £4) + (30,000 \times £8)}{100,000 \text{ units}}$$

$$= £5.20$$

The sum of the product break-even points is less than the break-even point for the company as a whole. It is incorrect to add the product break-even points because the sales mix will be different from the planned sales mix. The sum of the product break-even points assumes a sales mix of 50% to X and 50% to Y. The break-even point for the company as a whole assumes a planned sales mix of 70% to X and 30% to Y. CVP analysis will yield correct results only if the planned sales mix is equal to the actual sales mix.

Answer to question 9.27

(a) (i)

Products	1	2	3	Total
1. Unit contribution	£1.31	£0.63	£1.87	
2. Specific fixed costs per unit	£0.49	£0.35	£0.62	
3. General fixed costs per unit	£0.46	£0.46	£0.46	
4. Sales volume (000s units)	98.2	42.1	111.8	252.1
5. Total contribution (1 × 4)	£128.642	£26.523	£209.066	£364.231
6. Total specific fixed costs (2 × 4)	£48.118	£14.735	£69.316	£132.169
7. Total general fixed costs (3 × 4)	£45.172	£19.366	£51.428	£115.966
8. Unit selling price	£2.92	£1.35	£2.83	
9. Total sales revenue (8 × 4)	£286.744	£56.835	£316.394	£659.973

$$\text{Average contribution per unit} = \text{Total contribution (£364.23 1)/sales volume (252.1)}$$
$$= £1.4448$$

$$\text{Average selling price per unit} = \text{Total sales revenue (£659.973)/sales volume (252.1)}$$
$$= £2.6179$$

$$\text{Break-even point (units)} = \frac{\text{Total fixed costs}}{\text{Average contribution per unit}}$$
$$= (£132.169 + £115.966)/£1.4448$$
$$= 171.743 \text{ units}$$

$$\text{Break-even point (sales value)} = 171.743 \text{ units} \times \text{average selling price (£2.6179)}.$$
$$= £449.606$$

Alternatively, the break-even point (sales value) can be calculated using the following formula:

$$\text{Break-even point} = \frac{\text{Fixed costs (132.169 + £115.966)}}{\text{Total contribution (£364.231)}} \times \text{Total sales (£659.973)}$$
$$= £449.606$$

It is assumed that the question requires the calculation of the break-even point to cover both general and specific fixed costs. An alternative answer would have been to present details of the break-even point to cover only specific fixed costs.

(ii) The planned sales mix for Product 2 that was used to calculate the break-even point in (i) is 42.1/252.1. Therefore the number of units of Product 2 at the break-even point is:

$$42.1/252.1 \times 171,743 \text{ units} = 28,681$$

(b) At the forecast sales volume the profit/contributions are as follows:

	£000s
Contributions to all fixed costs	26.523
Less specific fixed costs	14.735
Contribution to general fixed costs	11.788
Less share of general fixed costs	19.366
Net loss	7.578

Product 2 provides a contribution of £11,788 towards general fixed costs and, unless savings in general fixed costs in excess of £11,788 can be made if Product 2 is abandoned, it is still viable to produce Product 2. If the company ceases production of Product 2 it will lose a contribution of £11,788 and total profits will decline by £11,788. The company should investigate whether a greater contribution than £11,788 can be generated from the resources. If this is not possible the company should continue production of Product 2.

Answer to question 9.30

Task 1	£	£
Sales		2,106,000
Less variable cost of sales:		
Cost of beds	1,620,000	
Commission	210,600	
Transport	216,000	2,046,600
Contribution		59,400

Average contribution per bed sold = £59,400/5,400 = £11
Fixed costs (£8,450 + £10,000 + £40,000 + £40,000) = £98,450

$$\text{Break-even point (units)} = \frac{\text{Fixed costs (£98,450)}}{\text{Contribution per unit (£11)}} = 8,950 \text{ beds}$$

Average selling price per unit (£2,106,000/5,400 beds) = £390
Break-even point (sales revenue) = 8,950 beds at £390 = £3,490,500

Task 2
The letter should include the items listed in (a) to (e) below:

(a) Required contribution:

	£
Salary	36,550
Interest lost	15,000
Fixed costs shown in Task 1	98,450
	150,000
Less manager's salary saved	40,000
Total contribution	110,000

The minimum profit required to compensate for loss of salary and interest is £11,550 (£110,000 − £98,450 fixed costs).

(b) Required volume = Required contribution (£110,000)/Contribution per unit (£11) = 10,000 beds

(c) Average life of a bed = (9 years × 0.10) + (10 years × 0.60) + (11 years × 0.3) = 10.2 years

Total bed population = 44,880 households × 2.1 beds per market = 94,248

$$\text{Estimated annual demand} = \frac{94,248 \text{ beds}}{\text{Average replacement period (10.2 years)}}$$

$$= 9,240 \text{ beds}$$

(d) The proposal will not achieve the desired profit. Estimated annual sales are 9,240 beds but 10,000 beds must be sold to achieve the desired profit. The shortfall of 760 beds will result in profit being £8,360 (760 × £11) less than the desired profit.

(e) The estimate of maximum annual sales volume may prove to be inaccurate because of the following reasons:
   (i) The population of Mytown may differ from the sample population. For

example the population of Mytown might contain a greater proportion of elderly people or younger people with families. Either of these situations may result in the buying habits of the population of Mytown being different from the sample proportion.

(ii) The data is historic and does not take into account future changes such as an increase in wealth of the population, change in composition or a change in buying habits arising from different types of beds being marketed.

Task 3
This question requires a knowledge of the material covered in Chapter 10. Therefore you should delay attempting this question until you have understood the content of Chapter 10.

	A	B	C	Total
	£	£	£	
Selling price	240	448	672	
Unit purchase cost	130	310	550	
Carriage inwards	20	20	20	
Contribution	90	118	102	
Square metres per bed	3	4	5	
Contribution per square metre	£30	£29.50	£20.40	
Ranking	1	2	3	
Maximum demand	35	45	20	
Storage required (square metres)	105	180	100	385

Monthly sales schedule and statement of profitability:

	£	£
Contribution from sales of A (35 × £90)		3,150
Contribution from sales of B (45 × £118)		5,310
Contribution from sales of C (3^a × £102)		306
		8,766
Less specific avoidable fixed costs:		
Staff costs	3,780	
Departmental fixed overheads	2,000	5,780
Contribution to general fixed overheads		2,986
Less general fixed overheads		2,520
Departmental profit		466

Note:
[a] The balance of storage space available for Model C is 300 square metres less the amount allocated to A and B (285 metres) = 15 metres. This will result in the sales of 3 beds (15 metres/5 metres per bed).

Answer to question 9.32

(a)
		£000s
Period 2 sales volume at period 1 prices (1,108.1 × 100/105)	=	1,055.333
Period 1 sales volume at period 1 prices	=	902.000
Increase in sales attributable to sales volume		153.333
% increase in sales volume (153.333/902 × 100)	=	17%

(b) (i)
	£000s
Increase in sales attributable to sales volume	153.333
Contribution based on period 1 cost structure (60% of sales)	92.000
Fixed costs are assumed to be unaffected by volume changes	
Increase in profit attributable to volume	92.000

(b) (ii)

	Period 2 sales volume at period 1 prices and period 1 production methods £000s	Period 2 sales volume at period 1 prices and period 2 production methods £000s
Sales	1,055.333	1,055.333
Variable costs	422.133[a]	379.905[b]
Contribution	633.200	675.428
Fixed costs	490.500[c]	522.857[d]
Net profit	142.700	152.571

	£000
Reduction in variable costs arising from reorganization in production methods	42.228
Increase in fixed costs arising from reorganization in production methods	(32.357)
	9.871

Notes:
[a] Sales × period 1 contribution to sales ratio of 60%
[b] £398.9 × 100/105
[c] Fixed costs are assumed to be unaffected by changes in sales volume
[d] £549.0 × 100/105

(c) Required contribution = Period 2 fixed costs (£549,000) + Period 1 profit (£50,700) = £599,700. The contribution/sales ratio (profit–volume ratio) for period 2 is 64% (£709.2/£1,108.1). In other words each £1 sale generates £0.64 contribution. To generate a contribution of £599,700 sales revenue of £937,031 is required (£599,700/0.64).

(d) The formula for the break-even point in sales revenue is:

$$\frac{\text{Fixed costs}}{\text{Contribution/sales ratio}} \quad \text{or Fixed costs} \times \frac{\text{Sales}}{\text{Contribution}}$$

When sales revenue generates a contribution that is exactly equal to fixed costs break-even point is achieved. To determine this level of sales revenue fixed costs must be divided by the rate at which contribution is made per £1 of sales.

Answer to question 9.33

(a) *Analysis of semi-variable costs[a]:*

$$\text{Method A: Variable element} = \frac{\text{Increase in costs}}{\text{Increase in activity}} = \frac{£10,000}{100,000 \text{ copies}}$$

$$= £0.10 \text{ per copy}$$

Fixed element = Total semi-variable cost (£55,000) − variable cost (£35,000) at an activity level of 350,000 copies

Therefore Fixed element = £20,000

$$\text{Method B: Variable element} = \frac{\text{Increase in costs}}{\text{Increase in activity}} = \frac{£5,000}{100,000 \text{ copies}}$$

$$= £0.05 \text{ per copy}$$

Fixed element = Total semi-variable cost (£47,500) − variable costs (£17,500) at an activity level of 350,000 copies

Therefore Fixed element = £30,000

Note:
[a] The analysis is based on a comparison of total costs and activity levels at 350,000 and 450,000 copies per year.

Contribution per copy of new magazine:

	Method A £	Method B £
Selling price	1.00	1.00
Variable cost (given)	(0.55)	(0.50)
Variable element of semi-variable cost	(0.10)	(0.05)
Lost contribution from existing magazine	(0.05)	(0.05)
Contribution	0.30	0.40

Calculation of net increase in company profits:

	Method A			Method B		
Copies sold	500,000	400,000	600,000	500,000	400,000	600,000
Contribution per copy	30 p	30 p	30 p	40 p	40 p	40 p
Total contribution	£150,000	£120,000	£180,000	£200,000	£160,000	£240 000
Fixed costs[a]	£100,000	£100,000	£100,000	£150,000	£150,000	£150,000
Net increase in profit	£50,000	£20,000	£80,000	£50,000	£10,000	£90,000

Note:
[a] Method A = Specific fixed costs (£80,000) + Semi-variable element (£20,000) = £100,000
Method B = Specific fixed costs (£120,000) + Semi-variable element (£30,000) = £150,000

(b)

$$\text{Break-even point} = \frac{\text{Fixed costs}}{\text{Contribution per unit}}$$

Method A = £100,000/0.30 = 333,333 copies
Method B = £150,000/0.40 = 375,000 copies

The margin of safety is the difference between the anticipated sales and the break-even point sales:

Method A = 500,000 − 333,333 = 166,667 copies
Method B = 500,000 − 375,000 = 125,000 copies

(c) Method B has a higher break-even point and a higher contribution per copy sold. This implies that profits from Method B are more vulnerable to a decline in sales volume. However, higher profits are obtained with Method B when sales are high (see 600,000 copies in (B)).

The break-even point from the sale of the existing magazine is 160,000 copies (£80,000/£0.50) and the current level of monthly sales is 220,000 copies. Therefore sales can drop by 60,000 copies before break-even point is reached. For every 10 copies sold of the new publication, sales of the existing publication will be reduced by one copy. Consequently, if more than 600,000 copies of the new publication are sold, the existing magazine will make a loss. If sales of the new magazine are expected to consistently exceed 600,000 copies then the viability of the existing magazine must be questioned.

Answer to question 9.34

(a) (i) The opportunity costs of producing cassettes are the salary forgone of £1,000 per month and the rental forgone of £400 per month.

(ii) The consultant's fees and development costs represent sunk costs.

(b) The following information can be obtained from the report.

	£10 selling price	£9 selling price
Sales quantity	7,500–10,000 units	12,000–18,000 units
Fixed costs[a]	£13,525	£17,525
Profit at maximum sales[b]	£3,975	£4,975
Profit/(loss) at minimum sales[c]	(£400)	(£2,525)
Break-even point[d]	7,729 units	14,020 units
Margin of safety:		
Below maximum	2,271 units	3,980 units
Above minimum	229 units	2,020 units

Notes:
[a] Fixed production cost + £1,400 opportunity cost
[b] (10,000 units × £1.75 contribution) − £13,525 fixed costs = £3,975 profit
  (18,000 units × £1.25 contribution) − £17,525 fixed costs = £4,975 profit
[c] (7,500 units × £1.75 contribution) − £13,525 fixed costs = £400 loss
  (12,000 units × £1.25 contribution) − £17,525 fixed costs = £2,525 loss
[d] Fixed costs/contribution per unit

Conclusions:
- (i)   The £10 selling price is less risky than the £9 selling price. With the £10 selling price, the maximum loss is lower and the break-even point is only 3% above minimum sales (compared with 17% for a £9 selling price).
- (ii) The £9 selling price will yield the higher profits if maximum sales quantity is achieved.
- (iii) In order to earn £3,975 profits at a £9 selling price, we must sell 17,200 units (required contribution of 17,525 fixed costs plus £3,975 divided by a contribution per unit of £1.25).

Additional information required:
- (i)   Details of capital employed for each selling price.
- (ii) Details of additional finance required to finance the working capital and the relevant interest cost so as to determine the cost of financing the working capital.
- (iii) Estimated probability of units sold at different selling prices.
- (iv) How long will the project remain viable?
- (v)   Details of range of possible costs. Are the cost figures given in the question certain?

Measuring costs and benefits for decision-making

Answers to Chapter 10

Question summary

10.1 to 10.7
Multiple choice questions.

10.8
Make-or-buy decisions.

10.9
Determining minimum short-term acceptable selling price.

10.10 and 10.11
Comparing relevant costs with a proposed pricing quotation.

10.12
Decision on which of two mutually exclusive contracts to accept.

10.13
Decision on whether a project involving sunk and opportunity costs should be continued.

10.14 and 10.15
Determination of minimum short-run selling price adopting a relevant cost approach.

10.16 to 10.18
These questions involve deleting a segment or product abandonment decisions. Question 10.17 also involves cost–volume–profit (CVP) analysis.

10.19
A recommendation as to whether to launch a new product.

10.20 to 10.22
Determining an optimal production schedule where a limiting factor applies.

10.23
Make-or-buy decisions and limiting factors.

10.24
Allocation of shop space based on limiting factors.

10.25
A make-or-buy decisions and limiting factors

10.26
Limiting/key factors and a decision relating to whether it is profitable to expand output by overtime.

10.27
Price/output and key factor decisions.

10.28
Limiting factor optimum production and the use of simultaneous equations where more than one scarce factor exists.

10.29
Computation of minimum and optimum selling prices based on price/demand relationships.

Answer to question 10.1

	X	Y	Z
Contribution per unit	£41	£54	£50
Kg used (Limiting factor)	2 (£10/5)	1	3
Contribution per kg	£20.5	£54	£16.67
Ranking	2	1	3

Answer = B

Answer to Question 10.2

The material is in regular use and if used will have to be replaced at a cost of £1,950 (600 × £3.25). The cash flow consequences are £1,950.

Answer = D

Answer to question 10.3

The shadow price is the opportunity cost or contribution per unit of a scarce resource.

	Quone	Qutwo
Contribution per unit	£8	£8.50
Kg per unit	3 (£6/£2)	2.50 (£5/£2)
Contribution per kg	£2.67	£3.40

Scarce materials will be used to make Qutwos and will yield a contribution of £3.40 per kg. Therefore the opportunity cost is £3.40 per kg.

Answer = D

Answer to question 10.4

Assuming that fixed costs will remain unchanged whether or not the company makes or buys the components the relevant cost of manufacture will be the variable cost. Under these circumstances the company should only purchase components if the purchase price is less than the variable cost. Therefore the company should only purchase component T.

Answer = D

Answer to question 10.5

(i) General fixed overheads are recovered at a rate of 80% of direct labour cost (£1.20/£1.50). Therefore general fixed overheads for Product M2 are £0.80 (80% × £1 Direct Labour Cost). The balance of £0.20 represents specific fixed costs for Product M2. The incremental costs of manufacturing are:

	Product M1 £	Product M2 £
Direct costs	4.60	4.40
Specified fixed costs		0.20
Maximum purchase price	4.60	4.60

Answer = B

(ii) General fixed overheads = £12,000 allocated to M1 (10,000 × £1.20)
= £10,000 allocated to M2 (12,500 × £1 less £2,500 specific fixed costs)

£22,000

$$\text{Number of units to be sold} = \frac{\text{Fixed costs } (£22,000) + \text{Desired profit } (£50,000)}{\text{Unit contribution } (£5.40)}$$

= 13,333 units

Answer = C

Answer to question 10.6

Incremental cost of new employees = £40,000 × 4 = £160,000
Supervision is not an incremental cost.

Incremental costs of retraining
= £15,000 + £100,000 replacement cost = £115,000
Retraining is the cheaper alternative and therefore the relevant cost of the contract is £115,000.

Answer = B

Answer to question 10.7

	Z1	Z2	Z3
Product contributions	£8	£7	£4.30
Contribution per £1 of labour	£4 (£8/£2)	£1.75	£2.40
Ranking	1	3	2

Answer = D

Answer to question 10.8

(a)

	£
Purchase price of component from supplier	50
Additional cost of manufacturing (variable cost only)	34
Savings if component manufactured	16

The component should be manufactured provided the following assumptions are correct:

(i)   Direct labour represents the additional labour cost of producing the component.

(ii) The company will not incur any additional fixed overheads if the component is manufactured.

(iii) There are no scarce resources. Therefore the manufacture of the component will not restrict the production of other more profitable products.

(b)   (i)   Additional fixed costs of £56,000 will be incurred, but there will be a saving in purchasing costs of £16 per unit produced. The break-even point is 3,500 units (fixed costs of £56,000/£16 per unit saving). If the quantity of components manufactured per year is less than 3,500 units then it will be cheaper to purchase from the outside supplier.

(ii) The contribution per unit sold from the existing product is £40 and each unit produced uses 8 scarce labour hours. The contribution per labour hour is £5. Therefore if the component is manufactured, 4 scarce labour hours will be used, resulting in a lost contribution of £20. Hence the relevant cost of manufacturing the components is £54, consisting of £34 incremental cost plus a lost contribution of £20. The component should be purchased from the supplier.

(c)   The book value of the equipment is a sunk cost and is not relevant to the decision whether the company should purchase or continue to manufacture the components. If we cease production now, the written-down value will be written off in a lump sum, whereas if we continue production, the written-down value will be written off over a period of years. Future cash outflows on the equipment will not be affected by the decision to purchase or continue to manufacture the components. For an illustration of the irrelevance of the written down value of assets for decision-making purposes see the section on replacement of equipment in Chapter 10.

Answer to question 10.12

(a)

	North East £	South coast £
Material X from stock (1)	19,440	
Material Y from stock (2)		49,600
Firm orders of material X (3)	27,360	
Material X not yet ordered (4)	60,000	
Material Z not yet ordered (5)		71,200
Labour (6)	86,000	110,000
Site management (7)	–	–
Staff accommodation and travel for site management (8)	6,800	5,600
Plant rental received (9)	(6,000)	–
Penalty clause (10)		28,000
	193,600	264,400
Contract price	288,000	352,000
Net benefit	94,400	87,600

(b) (1) If material X is not used on the North East contract the most beneficial use is to use it as a substitute material thus avoiding future purchases of £19,440 (0.9 × 21,600). Therefore by using the stock quantity of material X the company will have to spend £19,440 on the other materials.

(2) Material Y is in common use and the company should not dispose of it. Using the materials on the South coast contract will mean that they will have to be replaced at a cost of £49,600 (£24,800 × 2). Therefore the future cash flow impact of taking on the contract is £49,600.

(3) It is assumed that with firm orders for materials it is not possible to cancel the purchase. Therefore the cost will occur whatever future alternative is selected. The materials will be used as a substitute material if they are not used on the contract and therefore, based on the same reasoning as point 1 above, the relevant cost is the purchase price of the substitute material (0.9 × £30,400).

(4) The material has not been ordered and the cost will only be incurred if the contract is undertaken. Therefore additional cash flows of £60,000 will be incurred if the company takes on the North East contract.

(5) The same principles apply here as were explained in point 4 and additional cash flows of £71,200 will be incurred only if the company takes on the South coast contract.

(6) It is assumed that labour is an incremental cost and therefore relevant.

(7) The site management function is performed by staff at central head-quarters. It is assumed that the total company costs in respect of site management will remain unchanged in the short term whatever contracts are taken on. Site management costs are therefore irrelevant.

(8) The costs would be undertaken only if the contracts are undertaken. Therefore they are relevant costs.

(9) If the North East contract is undertaken the company will be able to hire out surplus plant and obtain a £6,000 cash inflow.

(10) If the South coast contract is undertaken the company will have to withdraw from the North East contract and incur a penalty cost of £28,000.

(11) The headquarter costs will continue whichever alternative is selected and they are not relevant costs.

(12) It is assumed that there will be no differential cash flows relating to notional interest. However, if the interest costs associated with the contract differ then they would be relevant and should be included in the analysis.

(13) Depreciation is a sunk cost and irrelevant for decision-making.

Answer to question 10.15

(a) *Calculation of minimum selling price:*

	£
Direct materials: Steel[a]	55.00
Brass Fittings[b]	20.00
Direct Labour: Skilled[c]	300.00
Semi-skilled[d]	–
Overhead[e]	7.50
Estimating time[f]	–
Administration[g]	–
Relevant cost of the order	382.50

Notes:

[a] Using the materials for the order will result in them having to be replaced. Therefore future cash outflows will increase by £55.

[b] Future cash outflows of £20 will be incurred.

[c] The required labour hours can be obtained by reducing production of another product involving a lost contribution before deducting the labour cost of £21 (£13 + £8) per hour (note that the labour cost will be incurred for all alternatives and therefore is not an incremental cash flow). Alternatively, the company can pay additional wages involving overtime of £300 (25 hours × £12). Therefore the latter course of action is the most economical and the incremental cash flows from undertaking the order will be £300.

[d] No incremental cost is involved since the alternative is paid idle time.

[e] The only incremental cost is power consisting of 10 hours at £0.75 per hour.

[f] Estimating time is a sunk cost.

[g] Administration does not involve any incremental cash flows.

(b) Factors to be considered include:
    (i) time period for repeat orders, the number of repeat orders and the likely demand;
    (ii) the cash flows generated from the alternative use of the capacity;
    (iii) competition to obtain future orders from Exe plc;
    (iv) estimated price quotations from competitors.

(c) *Limiting factor presentation:*

	Product X	Product Y
Product contribution	£10	£20
Kg of material used per product	1	4
Contribution per kg	£10	£5

Thus scarce materials should be allocated to Product X since it yields a contribution of £5 per kg in excess of the contribution derived from Product Y.

Opportunity cost approach:

	Product X	Product Y
Product contribution at acquisition cost	£10	£20
Lost contribution from alternative use:		
1 kg allocated to Y at £5 per kg	(£5)	
4 kg allocated to X at £10 per kg		£40
Cash flow impact per product	+£5	−£20
Cash flow impact per kg	+£5 (£5/1 kg)	−£5 (£20/4 kg)

The above analysis shows that X yields a contribution of £5 per kg when taking alternative uses of the materials into consideration. Producing Product Y results in the contribution being reduced by £5 per kg taking into account the alternative use of the materials. This is consistent with the limiting factor approach which indicates that the company is £5 per kg better off using the materials for X or £5 per kg worse off from using the materials on Y.

Answer to question 10.16

(a) (i)

Product	A	B	C
	£	£	£
Selling price	15	12	11
Less variable costs:			
Materials	(5)	(4)	(3)
Labour	(3)	(2)	(1.5)
Variable overhead (1)	(3.50)	(2)	(1.5)
Contribution	3.50	4	5

Note:
(1) Fixed overheads are apportioned to products on the basis of sales volume and the remaining overheads are variable with output.

(ii)

Product	B	C
	£	£
Selling price	12	9.50
Less variable costs:		
Materials	(4)	(3)
Labour	(2)	(1.80)
Variable overhead	(2)	(1.50)
Contribution	4	3.20

(b)　(i)

Product	A	B	C	Total
Total contribution	350,000	480,000	400,000	1,230,000
Less fixed costs:				
Labour				(220,000)
Fixed administration				(900,000)
Profit				110,000

(ii)

Product		B	C	Total
Total contribution^a		480,000	576,000	1,056,000
Less fixed costs:				
Labour^b				(160,000)
Fixed administration^c				(850,000)
Profit				46,000

Notes:

[a] B = 120,000 units × £4 contribution, C = 180,000 units × £3.20 contribution.

[b] (25% × £320,000 for B) plus (25% × £160,000 × 2 for C).

[c] Fixed administration costs will decline by $\frac{1}{6}$ of the amount apportioned to Product A (100/300 × £900,000). Therefore fixed overheads will decline from £900,000 to £850,000.

(c) Product A should not be eliminated even though a loss is reported for this product. If Product A is eliminated the majority of fixed costs allocated to it will still continue and will be borne by the remaining products. Product A generates a contribution of £350,000 towards fixed costs but the capacity released can be used to obtain an additional contribution from Product C of £176,000 (£576,000 − £400,000). This will result in a net loss in contribution of £174,000. However, fixed cost savings of £110,000 (£50,000 administration apportioned to Product A plus £100,000 labour for A less an extra £40,000 labour for Product C) can be obtained if Product A is abandoned. Therefore there will be a net loss in contribution of £64,000 (£174,000 − £110,000) and profits will decline from £110,000 to £64,000.

Answer to question 10.17

(a) (i)

	Product I £000	Product II £000	Product III £000	Total £000
Sales	2,475	3,948	1,520	7,943
Contribution	1,170	1,692	532	3,394
Attributable fixed costs	(275)	(337)	(296)	(908)
General fixed costs[a]	(520)	(829)	(319)	(1,668)
	(795)	(1,166)	(615)	(2,576)
Profit	375	526	(83)	818
	= £1.6/unit	= £1.40/unit	= (£0.04/unit)	

Note:
[a] General fixed costs are allocated to products at 21% of total sales revenue (£1,668/£7,943)

(ii) If Product III is discontinued it is assumed that variable costs and attributable (i.e. specific) fixed costs are avoidable. It is assumed that general fixed costs are common and unavoidable to all products and will remain unchanged if Product III is discontinued. However, it is possible that some general fixed costs may be avoidable in the longer term. The revised profits if Product III is discontinued will be:

	£000s
Contribution of Products I and II (£1,170 + £1,692)	2,862
Attributable fixed costs (£275 + £337)	(612)
General fixed costs	(1,668)
Profit	582

Profits will decline by £236,000 (£818 − £582) if Product III is discontinued because A Ltd will no longer obtain a contribution of £236,000 (£532 − £296) towards general fixed costs.

(iii) Extra sales of 15,385 units (£80,000 additional fixed costs/£5.20 unit contribution) will be required to cover the additional advertising expenditure. It is assumed that existing fixed costs will remain unchanged.

(iv) The revised unit contribution will be £3.45 (£9.45 – £6).

$$\text{Required sales} = \frac{£1,692,000 \text{ (existing total contribution)}}{£3.45 \text{ revised unit contribution}}$$

= 490,435 units (an increase of 30.4% over the budgeted sales of 376,000 units)

(b) The following factors will influence cost behaviour in response to changes in activity:

(i) The magnitude of the change in activity (more costs are likely to be affected when there is a large change in activity).

(ii) Type of expense (some expenses are directly variable with volume such as direct materials, whereas others are fixed or semi-fixed).

     (iii) Management policy (some expenses are varied at the discretion of management, e.g. advertising).

     (iv) The time period (in the long term, all costs can be changed in response to changes in activity whereas in the short term, some costs, e.g. salaries of supervisors, will remain unchanged).

Answer to question 10.18

(a)   Company gross profit % = 38% (£3,268/£8,600 × 100)

     Therefore Division 5 gross profit % = 19%

Division 5 sales	= £860,000 (10% × £8.6m)
Division 5 gross profit	= £163,400 (19% × £860,000)
Division 5 contribution	= £479,400 (£316,000 + £163,400)

The situation for the year ahead if the division were not sold would be as follows:

Contribution	= £527,340 (£479,400 × 1.1)
Less avoidable fixed costs	= £455,700 [£316,000 +
	(£156,000 − £38,000)] × 1.05
Add contribution from other divisions	= £20,000
Expected profit	£91,640

If Division 5 were sold, the capital sum would yield a return of £75,400. Therefore the decision on the basis of the above information should be not to sell Division 5.

(b)   Other factors that should influence the decision include:

     (i) The need to focus on a longer-term time horizon. A decision based solely on the year ahead is too short and ignores the long-term impact from selling Division 5.

     (ii) The impact on the morale of the staff working in other divisions arising from the contraction of activities and the potential threat of redundancies.

     (iii) Alternative use of the resources currently deployed in Division 5 instead of their current use.

(c)   If Division 5 is sold, the capital sum would yield a return of £75,000, but a contribution of £20,000 is lost. Consequently, a profit of £55,000 is required. The required contribution is therefore £510,700 (£55,000 + £455,700) and the percentage increase required is 6.5% (£510,700/£479,400 − 100%).

Answer to question 10.20

(a)

	Chairs	Benches	Tables	Total
Timber required per unit (m^2)	2.5(£5/£2)	7.5(£15/£2)	5(£10/£2)	
Budgeted sales volume (units)	4,000	2,000	1,500	
Total timber required (m^2)	10,000	15,000	7,500	32,500

Production requirements exceed the available supply of materials by 12,500 m^2

	Chairs	Benches	Tables
Unit contributions (£)	8	17.50	16
Timber requirements (m^2)	2.5	7.5	5
Contribution per m^2 (£)	3.2	2.33	3.20
Ranking	1	3	1

The scarce materials should be allocated as follows:

	Materials used	Balance unused
Chairs (4,000 units × 2.5)	10,000	10,000
Tables (1,500 units × 5)	7,500	2,500
Benches (2,500/7.5 = 333 units)	2,500	–

The above production plan is sufficient to meet the order that has already been accepted. The profit arising from the above production plan is calculated as follows:

	£
Chairs (4,000 units × £8 contribution)	32,000
Tables (1,500 units × £16 contribution)	24,000
Benches (333 units × £17.50 contribution)	5,827
Total contribution	61,827
Fixed overheads (4,000 × £4.50) + (2,000 × £11.25) + (1,500 × £9)	54,000
Profit	7,827

(b) The above production plan indicates that maximum sales demand for chairs and tables has been met but there is unutilized demand for benches. Therefore any additional materials purchased will be used to make benches yielding a contribution per unit sold of £17.50 and contribution per metre of material used of £2.33 (see part (a) for calculation). The company should not pay above £2.33 in excess of the acquisition cost of materials. The maximum purchase price is £4.33 (£2 + £2.33).

(c) See Chapter 2 for an explanation of each of the items listed in the question.

Answer to question 10.21

(a) (i)

Product	X		Y		Z	
	£	£	£	£	£	£
Direct materials		50		120		90
Variable ovhead		12		7		16
Direct labour:						
Department A	70		40		75	
Department B	24		18		30	
Department C	32	126	16	74	60	165
Variable production cost		188		201		271
Sales price		210		220		300

				Total
Unit contribution	22	19	29	£
Total contribution	165,000	114,000	174,000	453,000
Fixed costs				300,000
Profit				153,000

(ii) Department B labour hours limitation:

Product X 30,000 hours (7,500 × 4 hours)

    Y 18,000 hours (6,000 × 3 hours)

    Z 30,000 (6,000 × 5 hours)

    78,000 hours

Products	X	Y	Z
Unit contribution	£22	£19	£29
Department B labour hours	4	3	5
Contribution per Department B hour	£5.50	£6.33	£5.80
Ranking	3	1	2

Maximum sales are 9,000 units of X (7,500 × 1.20), 7,500 units of Y (6,000 × 1.25) and 8,000 of Z (6,000 × 1.33). Using the above rankings the optimal product mix is:

Product	Units sold	Department B hours used	Contribution £
Y	7,500	22,500	142,500
Z	8,000	40,000	232,000
X	3,875 (15,500/4)	15,500	85,250
		78,000	459,750
Less fixed costs			300,000
Profit			159,750

(iii) Factors to be considered which have not been taken into account in the above analysis include:

1. The impact on customer goodwill. Some customers may buy all three products and they may choose to buy elsewhere if their supply of Product X is restricted. Also the company may permanently lose Product X customers if the supply is restricted.
2. Competitors' reactions. If supply of Product X is restricted, competitors may exploit the situation by stressing that they are able to meet demand for Product X and look after their customers and provide a better service.
3. Some of the fixed costs may be attributable to specific products and avoidable if output is reduced. When avoidable fixed costs are taken into account the product mix specified in (a) (ii) may not be the optimum mix.

(b) Linear programming should be used. This technique enables an objective function to be maximized (e.g. contribution) subject to meeting the requirements of more than one input constraint.

Answer to question 10.23

(a)

	Component 12	Component 14	Product VW	Product XY
Variable cost	42	32	30	64
Purchase price	60	30		
Selling price			33	85
Decision	Make	Buy	Sell	Sell

The assumptions on which the above advice is based are:
- (i) Variable costs will vary with units produced and are constant per unit of output.
- (ii) Direct labour is assumed to be a variable cost and not a fixed cost.
- (iii) No limiting factors exist, and the company does not have any capacity constraints which might result in the need to consider opportunity costs.
- (iv) Fixed costs are common and unavoidable to all alternatives, and therefore will not change.
- (v) No additional cost will be incurred if the component is purchased – for example. additional inspection and ordering costs.
- (vi) Quality and delivery will be satisfactory.
- (vii) The facilities cannot be used for more profitable alternatives.

(b)

	Component 12	Component 14	Product VW	Product XY	Total
Machine time per unit (hrs)	8	Buy	6	12	
Production (units)	7,000		5.000	4,000	
Machine hours required	56,000		30,000	48,000	134,000ª
Contribution/cost saving (£)	18 (60 − 42)		3	21	
Contribution per machine hour (£)	2.25		0.50	1.75	
Ranking	1		3	2	

The company should produce 7,000 units of component 12. This requires 56,000 machine hours. The remaining 24,000 machine hours should be used to produce 2,000 units of product XY.

Note:
ª 80,000 machine hours are available. Therefore machine hours are the limiting factor.

Answer to question 10.27

Task 1
(a) and (b)

Selling price	£60	£70	£80	£90
Sales volume (units)	25,000	20,000	16,000	11,000
	£ per unit	£ per unit	£ per unit	£ per unit
Direct material	14.00	14.00	14.00	16.10 (£14 × 115/100)
Direct labour	13.00	13.00	11.70 (90%)	11.70
Variable production overhead	4.00	4.00	4.00	4.00
Sales commission (10% of selling price)	6.00	7.00	8.00	9.00
Total variable cost per unit	37.00	38.00	37.70	40.80
Contribution per unit	23.00	32.00	42.30	49.20

	£000	£000	£000	£000
Total contribution	575	640	676.8	541.2
Fixed costs:				
production overhead (25,000 × £8)	200	200	190	190
selling and distribution (25,000 × £3)	75	70	70	70
administration (25,000 × £2)	50	50	50	50
Total fixed costs	325	320	310	310
Total annual profit	250	320	366.8	231.2

Task 2

(a) A selling price of £80 maximizes company profits at £366,800 per annum.

(b) Factors to be considered include:

(i) The effect on morale arising from a large reduction in direct labour and the resulting redundancies.

(ii) If competitors do not increase their prices customers may migrate to competitors in the long term and long-term annual profits may be considerably less than the profits predicted in the above schedule. The migration of customers may also enable competitors to reap the benefits of economies of scale thus resulting in their having lower unit costs than Rane Ltd.

Task 3

(a) The products should first he ranked according to their contribution per component used.

	Product A	Product B	Product C	Product D
	£ per unit	£ per unit	£ per unit	£ per unit
Selling price	14	12	16	17
Variable costs	11	11	12	12
Contribution	3	1	4	5
Number of components used per unit	2 (£4/£2)	1 (£2/£2)	3 (£6/£2)	4 (£8/£2)
Contribution per component	£1.50	£1.00	£1.33	£1.25
Ranking	1	4	2	3

The scarce components should be allocated as follows:

Product	Units	Components used	Balance unused
A	4,000	8,000	14,400
C	3,600	10,800	3,600
D	900	3,600	–
		22,400	

(b) Profit to be earned next period:

Product	Units	Contribution per unit	Total
		£	£
A	4,000	3	12,000
C	3.600	4	14,400
D	900		4,500
Total contribution			30,900
Fixed costs			8,000
Profit			22,900

Answer to question 10.28

(a)

		Product X	Product Y	Total
(1)	Estimated demand (000 units)	315	135	
(2)	Machine hours required (per 000 units)	160	280	
(3)	Machine hours required to meet demand			
	(1×2)	50,400	37,800	88,200

The machine hours required to meet demand are in excess of the machine hours that are available. Therefore machine hours are the limiting factor and the company should allocate capacity according to contribution per machine hour.

	Product X	Product Y
	£	£
Selling price	11.20	15.70
Variable cost	6.30	8.70
Contribution	4.90	7.00
Machine hours required per unit[a]	0.16	0.28
Contribution per machine hour	£30.625	£25

Note:
[a] Product X = 160/1,000   Product Y = 280/1,000

The company should concentrate on maximizing output of Product X. Meeting the maximum demand of Product X will require 50,400 machine hours and this will leave 34,600 hours (85,000 hrs − 50,400 hrs) to be allocated to Product Y. Therefore 123,571 units (34,600 hrs/0.28 hrs) of Y and 315,000 units of X should be produced.

(b)

	Product X	Product Y	Total
	£	£	£
Contribution per unit	4.90	7.00	
Sales volume	315,000	123,571	
Contribution (£000s)	1,543.5	864.997	2,408.497
Less fixed costs[a]			2,124.997
Profit			283.500

Note:

[a] Fixed costs: Product X = 315,000 units × £4 per unit	= £1,260,000
Product Y = 123,571 units × £7 per unit	= £864,997
	2,124,997

(c) There are now two limiting factors and linear programming techniques must be used.

Let   X = Number of units of X produced (in 000s of units)
      Y = Number of units of Y produced (in 000s of units)

$160X + 280Y = 85,000$ Machine hours	(1)
$120X + 140Y = 55,000$ Labour hours	(2)

Multiply equation (2) by 2 and equation (1) by 1

$160X + 280Y = 85,000$ (1)
$240X + 280Y = 110,000$ (2)

Subtract equation (2) from equation (1)

$-80X = -25,000$
$X = 312.5$ (i.e. 312,500 units)

Substitute for X in equation (1)

$160 (312.5) + 280Y = 85,000$
$50,000 + 280Y = 85,000$
$280Y = 35,000$
$Y = 125$ (i.e. 125,000)

Therefore the optimal output to fully utilize both labour and machine capacity is 312,500 units of Product X and 125,000 units of Product Y.

Activity-based costing

Answers to Chapter 11

Question summary

ABC did not emerge until the late 1980s, and therefore very few examination questions have been set on this topic. This chapter contains five questions:

11.1 and 11.2
Essay questions.

11.3 and 11.7
A comparison of product costs derived from traditional and activity-based costing is required. Question 11.6 also requires the preparation of conventional costing and ABC costing profit statements.

Answer to question 11.2

The answer to the question should describe the two-stage overhead allocation process and indicate that most cost systems use direct labour hours in the second stage. In today's production environment direct labour costs have fallen to about 10% of total costs for many firms and it is argued that direct labour is no longer a suitable base for assigning overheads to products. Using direct labour encourages managers to focus on reducing direct labour costs when they represent only a small percentage of total costs.

Approaches which are being adopted include:

(i) Changing from a direct labour overhead-recovery rate to recovery methods based on machine time. The justification for this is that overheads are caused by machine time rather than direct labour hours and cost.

(ii) Implementing activity-based costing systems that use many different cost drivers in the second stage of the two-stage overhead allocation procedure.

The answer should then go on to describe the benefits of ABC outlined in Chapter 11. Attention should also be drawn to the widespread use of direct labour hours by Japanese companies. According to Hiromoto[a] Japanese companies allocate overhead costs using the direct labour cost/hours to focus design engineers' attention on identifying opportunities to reduce the products' labour content. They use direct labour to encourage designers to make greater use of technology because this frequently improves long-term competitiveness by increasing quality, speed and flexibility of manufacturing.

Note:
[a] Hiromoto, T. (1988) Another hidden edge – Japanese Management Accounting, *Harvard Business Review*, July–August, pp. 22–6.

Answer to question 11.4

(a) Total machine hours = 120 × 4 hrs) + (100 × 3 hrs) + (80 × 2 hrs) + (120 × 3 hrs)
   = 1,300hrs

$$\text{Machine hour overhead rate} = \frac{£10,430 + £5,250 + £3,600 + £2,100 + £4,620}{1,300 \text{ hours}}$$

   = £20 per machine hour

Product	A	B	C	D
	£	£	£	£
Direct material	40	50	30	60
Direct labour	28	21	14	21
Overheads at £20 per machine hour	80	60	40	60
	148	131	84	114
Units of output	120	100	80	120
Total cost	£17,760	£13,100	£6,720	£16,920

(b) *Costs:*

	£	Cost driver	Cost driver transactions	Cost per unit £
Machine department	10,430	Machine hours	1,300 hours	8.02
Set-up costs	5,250	Production runs	21	250
Stores receiving	3,600	Requisitions raised	80 (4 × 20)	45
Inspection/quality control	2,100	Production runs	21	100
Materials handling	4,620	Number of orders executed	42	110

Note:
Number of production runs = Total output (420 units)/20 units per set-up.
Number of orders executed = Total output (420 units/10 units per order.
The total costs for each product are computed by multiplying the cost driver rate per unit by the quantity of the cost driver consumed by each product.

	A		B		C	D
Prime costs	8,160	(£68 × 120)	7,100		3,520	9,720
Set ups	1,500	(£250 × 6)	1,250	(£250 × 5)	1,000	1,500
Stores/receiving	900	(£45 × 20)	900		900	900
Inspection/quality	600	(£100 × 6)	500		400	600
Handling despatch	1,320	(£110 × 12)	1,100	(£110 × 10)	880	1,320
Machine dept cost[a]	3,851		2,407		1,284	2,888
Total costs	16,331		13,257		7,984	16,928

Note:
[a] A = 120 units × 4 hrs × £8.02: B = 100 units × 3 hrs × £8.02

(c) *Cost per unit:*

Costs from (a)	148.00	131.00	84.00	141.00
Costs from (b)	136.0	132.57	99.80	141.07
Difference	(11.91)	1.57	15.80	0.07

Product A is over-costed with the traditional system. Products B and C are under-costed and similar costs are reported with Product D. It is claimed that ABC more accurately measures resources consumed by products (see the section on an illustration of ABC and traditional product costing systems in Chapter 11). Where cost-plus pricing is used, the transfer to an ABC system will result in different product prices. If activity-based costs are used for stock valuations then stock valuations and reported profits will differ.

Answer to question 11.6

(a) (i) *Conventional Absorption Costing Profit Statement:*

		XYI	YZT	ABW
(1)	Sales volume (000 units	50	40	30
		£	£	£
(2)	Selling price per unit	45	95	73
(3)	Prime cost per unit	32	84	65
(4)	Contribution per unit	13	11	8
(5)	Total contribution in £000s (1 × 4)	650	440	240
(6)	Machine department overheads[a]	120	240	144
(7)	Assembly department overheads[b]	288.75	99	49.5
	Profit (£000s)	241.25	101	46.5

Total profit = £388,750

Notes:
[a] XYI = 50,000 × 2 hrs x £1.20, YZT = 40,000 × 5 hrs × £1.20
[b] XYI = 50,000 × 7 hrs x £0.825, YZT = 40,000 × 3 hrs × £0.825

(ii) *Cost pools:*

	Machining services	Assembly services	Set-ups	Order processing	Purchasing
£000	357	318	26	156	84
Cost drivers	420,000 machine hours	530,000 direct labour hours	520 set-ups	32,000 customer orders	11,200 suppliers' orders
Cost driver rates	£0.85 per machine hour	£0.60 direct labour hour	£50 per set-up	£4.875 per customer order	£7.50 per suppliers' order

ABC Profit Statement:

	XYI £000s	YZT £000s	ABW £000s
Total contribution	650	440	240
Less overheads:			
Machine department at £0.85 per hour	85	170	102
Assembly at £0.60 per hour	210	72	36
Set-up costs at £50 per set-up	6	10	10
Order processing at £4.875 per order	39	39	78
Purchasing at £7.50 per order	22.5	30	31.5
Profit (Loss)	287.5	119	(17.5)

Total profit = £389,000

(b) See the section on a comparison of ABC and traditional product costs in Chapter 11 for the answer to this question.

Capital investment decisions

Answers to Chapter 12

Question summary

12.1
Payback and NPV calculations.

12.2
Calculation of internal rate of return (IRR) with equal annual cash flows.

12.3
Calculation of accounting rate of return and NPV.

12.4
Part (a) requires the calculation of the NPV and the payback period. Part (b) is concerned with a machine replacement decision. The cost savings of replacing the machine are regarded as cash inflows and the revenues are considered to be irrelevant since they are the same for the existing and the replacement machine.

12.5
Calculation of NPV and payback.

12.6
Present value of purchasing or renting machinery.

12.7 to 12.11
These questions require the calculation of payback. accounting rate of return and net present value. and in most cases. require a recommendation as to which project should be accepted.

12.12
Computation of NPV and tax payable.

Answer to question 12.1

(a)   (i)   Annual cash flow = Annual profit + Annual depreciation (£15,000).
The annual cash flows for each project are as follows:

Year	Project 1	Project 2
1	45,000	40,000
2	45,000	30,000
3	35,000	35,000
4	5,000	35,000
5	5,000	0

$$\text{Payback period} = \frac{1 + 75 - 45}{45} \quad \frac{2 + 75 - 70}{35}$$

$$= 1.7 \text{ years} = 2.1 \text{ years}$$

(ii)

	Cash flow	Discount factor	Project 1 PV	Cash flow	Project 2 PV
	£		£	£	£
Outlay	(75,000)	1	(75,000)	(75,000)	(75,000)
Year 1	45,000	0.869	39,105	40,000	34,760
2	45,000	0.756	34,020	30,000	22,680
3	35,000	0.657	22,995	35,000	22,995
4	5,000	0.571	2,855	35,000	19,985
5	5,000	0.497	2,485	–	–
PV Inflows			£101,460		£100,420
NPV			£26,460		£25,420

(b)   See sections on the concept of NPV and payback methods in Chapter 12 for the answer to this question.

(c)   Both the NPV and payback methods indicate that the firm should choose Project 1.

Answer to question 12.2

(a)   The IRR is where:

annual cash inflows × discount factor = investment cost
i.e. £4,000 × discount factor = £14,000

$$\text{Therefore} \quad \text{discount factor} = \frac{£14,000}{£4,000}$$

$$= 3.5$$

We now work along the five-row table of the cumulative discount tables to find the discount rate with a discount factor closest to 3.5. This is 13%. Therefore the IRR is 13%.

(b) The annual saving necessary to achieve a 12% internal rate of return is where:

$$\text{annual savings} \times 12\% \text{ discount factor} = \text{investment cost}$$
$$\text{i.e. annual savings} \times 3.605 = £14,000$$
$$\text{Therefore annual savings} = \frac{£14,000}{3.605}$$
$$= £3,883$$

(c) NPV is calculated as follows:

	£
£4,000 received annually from years 1–5:	
£4,000 × 3.791 discount factor	15,164
Less investment cost	14,000
NPV	1,164

Answer to question 12.4

(a) This part of the question requires you to focus on the new machine only and does not require a decision as to which machine should be purchased. Depreciation should not be included in the analysis because it is already included in the investment cost. Allocated costs are not relevant costs. The net cash inflow per unit is £1.75 (£3 − £1.25).

	Net cash inflow £	Discount factor	Present value £
Year 1	70,000 (40,000 × £1.75)	0.833	58,310
2	70,000	0.694	48,580
3	52,500	0.579	30,398
4	35,000	0.482	16,870
5	35,000	0.402	14,070
			168.228
		Investment cost	(150,000)
		NPV	18,228

(i) Payback period: Cumulative cash inflows are £140,000 by the end of year 2 and a further £10,000 is required to repay the initial cost. Therefore the payback period is 2 years plus £10,000/£52,500 or 2.19 years.

(ii) NPV = £18.228.

(b) The cash inflows are represented by the savings in relevant operating costs of £0.25 per unit (£1.50 − £1.25) and the sale proceeds from the old machine of £130,000.

	Net cash inflow £	Discount factor	Present value £
Year 0	130,000	1.000	130,000
1	10,000 (40,000 × £0.25)	0.833	8,330
2	10,000	0.694	6,940
3	7,500	0.579	4,342

4	5,000		0.482		2,410
5	5,000		0.402		2,010
					154,032
			Investment cost		(150,000)
			NPV		4,032

(c) Factors to be considered:
   (i) The quality of fruit pies.
   (ii) The reliability and speed of delivery service.
   (iii) The possibility of future price increases.
   (iv) The number of suppliers. If there are few suppliers the group might be entirely dependent on the supplier who may take advantage of the situation.
   (v) The impact on the work force. Will there be any redundancies? Is there high unemployment in the area?

Answer to question 12.7

(a) The answer should describe the following stages:
   (i) *Initiation of proposals:* The originator of a proposal should make a request for a capital appropriation for those projects which would seem to have merit. The request should include a description of the proposal, the reasons for making it, and an estimate of the costs benefits and economic life.
   (ii) *Approval of the proposal:* A financial appraisal should be undertaken by the accounting staff and a system of approval should be established. A capital expenditure committee should be established and the committee should then be responsible for approving all major projects. Procedures should also be set for the approval at lower management levels of the less important projects.
   (iii) *Control:* Actual costs should be compared with estimated costs which were included in the project proposal. This process will provide an incentive for the proposers of future projects to make careful estimates and also provide an incentive to control costs and the date of completion. Comparisons should take place at periodic intervals during the installation and construction stage of the project. Reports should be prepared which give details of the percentage completion; the estimated costs to complete compared with the original estimate; the time taken compared to the estimate for the current stage of completion; and also the estimated completion date compared with the original estimate. This information will enable management to take corrective cost-saving action, such as changing the construction schedule. Every effort should be made to avoid a delay in completion because this can be expensive in terms of additional costs.
   (iv) *Post-audit:* A review of the project should be undertaken once it has been completed to evaluate the capital expenditure decision. This should involve a comparison of actual cash flows with budgeted cash flows.

(b) (i) Annual depreciation for both projects is £40,000 per annum (£200,000 − £40,000)/4 years. This is added back to profits to compute cash flows.

Project	X	Y
	£	£
Year 1 Cash flows	120,000	70,000
2	120,000	90,000
3	80,000	130,000
4	100,000	200,000

Payback periods:
Project X = 1 year + (£200,000 − £120,000)/£120,000
         = 1.67 years
Project Y = 2 years + (£200,000 − £160,000)/£130,000
         = 2.3 years

(ii) *Accounting rate of return:*

Project profits	X	Y
Year 1	80,000	30,000
2	80,000	50,000
3	40,000	90,000
4	20,000	120,000
	220,000	290,000
Number of years	4	4
Average profit	55,000	72,500

$$\text{Average investment} \quad \frac{200,000 + 40,000}{2} \quad \frac{200,000 + 40,000}{2}$$

$$= 120,000 \qquad = 120,000$$

$$\text{Accounting rate of return} \quad \frac{55,000}{120,000} \quad \frac{72,500}{120,000}$$

$$= 46\% \qquad = 60\%$$

(iii) *Discounted cash flow:*

		Project X Cash flow DCF	Project Y Cash flow DCF
Factor		£	£
0.862	Year 1	120,000 =103,440	70,000 = 60,340
0.743	2	120,000 = 89,160	90,000 = 66,870
0.641	3	80,000 = 51,280	130,000 = 83,330
0.552	4	100,000 = 55,200	200,000 =110,400
		299,080	320,940
Less initial investment		200,000	200,000
Net present value		99,080	120,940

(c) The answer should explain that the decision should be based on the NPV technique and justify the superiority of this method over the payback and accounting rate of return methods. (See Chapter 12 for an explanation.) Therefore Project Y should be selected.

(d) (i) See the section on the opportunity cost of an investment in Chapter 12 for an explanation of the cost of capital. The cost of capital is important because it represents the opportunity cost of shareholders' funds. Only those projects which yield a return in excess of the opportunity cost of capital should be accepted.

(ii) Risk can be taken into account by:

(1) increasing the discount rate for higher risk projects;

(2) using the payback method and, for high risk projects, accepting only those projects with short payback periods.

Answer to question 12.9

(a) The answer should stress that NPV is considered superior to the payback method and the accounting rate of return because it takes account of the time value of money. For a description of the time value of money you should refer to the sections on compounding and discounting and the concept of net present value in Chapter 12. The answer should also draw attention to the limitations of the payback method and accounting rate of return described in Chapter 12.

(b) (i) To compute the NPV it is necessary to convert the profits into cash flows by adding back depreciation of £25,000 per annum in respect of the asset purchased at the end of year 3 for £75,000. The NPV calculation is as follows:

Year	Cash flow £	Discount factor	NPV
3	(75,000)	0.675	(50,625)
4	35,000	0.592	20,720
5	28,000	0.519	14,532
6	27,000	0.465	12,555
			(2.818)

(b) (ii) The cash flows are based on the assumption that the reinvestment in R is not made at the end of year 3.

Year	Discount factor	Project T cash flows[a] £	Project T NPV £	Project R cash flows £	Project R NPV £
1	0.877	27,000	23,679	40,000[c]	35,080
2	0.769	30,000	23,070	45,000	34,605
3	0.675	32,000	21,600	45,000[d]	30,375
4	0.592	44,000	26,048		
5	0.519	40,000[b]	20,760		
			115,157		100,060
Investment outlay			70,000		60,000
NPV			45,157		40,060

Payback: T = 2 years + (£70,000 − £57,000)/£32,000 = 2.41 years
R = 1 year + (£60,000 − £40,000)/£45,000 = 1.44 years

The decision should be to invest in Project T because it has the higher NPV.

Notes:
[a] Yearly profits plus (£70,000 − £10,000)/5 years depreciation
[b] £18,000 profits + £12,000 depreciation + £10,000 sale proceeds
[c] Profits plus £60,000/3 years depreciation
[d] £75,000 investment outlay − £50,000 = Annual profit (£25,000). Cash flow = £25,000 profit + £20,000 depreciation.

(c) For an explanation of the meaning of the term 'discount rate' see the section on the opportunity cost of an investment in Chapter 12. The discount rate can be derived from observations of the returns shareholders require in financial markets. Where a project is to be financed fully by borrowing. the cost of borrowing could be used as a basis for determining the discount rate.

Answer to question 12.12

The report should include the information contained in items (a) to (c) below:

(a) Depreciation is not a cash flow. The operating net cash inflows (before tax) therefore consist of sales less materials and labour costs. The NPV calculation is as follows:

Year	0	1	2	3	4
	£	£	£	£	£
Net cash inflows before tax		80,000	75,000	69,750	
Tax[a]			(14,025)	(15,469)	4,826
Investment outlay	(150,000)				
Net cash flow	(150,000)	80,000	60,975	54,281	4,826
Discount factor (18%)	1.000	0.847	0.718	0.609	0.516
Present value	(150,000)	67,760	43,780	33,057	2,490

NPV = −£2,913

Note:
The tax computation is as follows:

Year	1	2	3
	£	£	£
Net cash inflows before tax	80,000	75,000	69,750
Writing down allowances	37,500	28,125	84,375
Taxable profit	42,500	46,875	(14,625)
Tax at 33%	14,025	15,469	(4,826)
Writing down allowances:			
Opening WDV	150,000	112,500	84,375
Writing down allowances (25%)	37,500	28,125	
Closing WDV	112,500	84,375	Nil
Balancing allowance			84,375

(b) Because corporation taxes are payable on taxable profits and not accounting profits depreciation has been replaced by the Inland Revenue's allowable depreciation (known as written-down allowances). The net cost of the asset is £150,000 and written-down allowances received amounted to £65,625

(£37,500 + £28,125). Therefore a balancing allowance is available at the end of the asset's life of £84,375 (£150,000 − £65,625). The Inland Revenue allows the net cost of the asset to be claimed over its life with a balancing adjustment in the final year. Because taxation is normally payable 9 months after the company's accounting year end the taxation cash flows are shown to be delayed by one year. This is a simplification of the actual situation but is normally sufficiently accurate for appraising investments.

(c) Other factors to be considered include:
  (i) The probability of obtaining a subsequent contract. There would be no need to purchase a further machine and the project would therefore yield a positive NPV.
  (ii) The negative NPV is very small and if the company has other profitable activities it may be worthwhile accepting in order to have the chance of obtaining a second contract and establishing long-term relationships with a large multinational customer.
  (iii) Capacity that is available. If other profitable opportunities have to be forgone to undertake the contract because of shortage of capacity then the opportunity cost should be included in the financial analysis.

The budgeting process

Answers to Chapter 13

Question summary

13.1 to 13.5
Multiple choice questions.

13.6 and 13.7
Discussion questions relating to budgeting.

13.8 to 13.14
Preparation of cash budgets. Question 13.14 is the most difficult. Question 13.8 also requires the preparation of the budgeted profit and loss account and balance sheet and 13.11 involves the calculation of stock, debtor and creditor balances.

13.15 to 13.20
Preparation of functional budgets. Question 13.19 also requires the calculation of sales to achieve a target profit and 13.20 involves the computation of a standard product cost.

13.21
Preparation of materials purchase and usage budget and journal entries for a standard costing system.

13.22
Preparation of functional budgets, cash budget and budgeted profit and loss account and balance sheet.

13.23
Calculation of the number of budgeted direct labour employees required to meet budgeted production plus the calculation of product direct labour costs.

13.24
Preparation of functional budgets and comments on sales forecasting methods.

13.25
Construction of a model in the form of equations for the preparation of a cash budget.

Answer to question 13.1

Answer = B

Answer to question 13.2

Answer = A

Answer to question 13.3

	£	£
Cash sales		22,000
Credit sales:		
April (70% × 0.6 × 0.98 × £70,000)	28,812	
March (27% × 0.6 × £60,000)	9,720	38,532
		60,532

Answer = C

Answer to question 13.4

Answer = C

Answer to question 13.5

Answer = B

Answer to question 13.8

(a)　(i)

Freewheel Ltd
Cash Budget July–December 1992

	July £	Aug. £	Sep. £	Oct. £	Nov. £	Dec. £
Opening balance	3,000	(1,500)	(1,600)	15,300	14,100	8,200
Receipts						
Sales						
Cash	13,500	13,800	14,400	20,000	15,200	12,000
Credit	12,000	12,600	13,500	13,800	14,400	20,000
Share issue			20,000			
	25,500	26,400	47,900	33,800	29,600	32,000

Expenses

Purchases	12,000	13,000	14,000	18,000	16,000	14,000
Wages and						
salaries (1)	6,000	7,500	7,500	7,500	9,000	9,000
(2)	2,000	2,000	2,500	2,500	2,500	3,000
Overheads	7,000	7,000	7,000	7,000	8,000	8,000
Fixed Asset						
Purchase						10,000
	27,000	29,500	31,000	35,000	35,500	44,000
Surplus/deficit	(1,500)	(3,100)	16,900	(1,200)	(5,900)	(12,000)
Closing balance	1,500	(1,600)	15,300	14,100	8,200	(3,800)

(ii)

Freewheel Ltd
Budgeted Profit and Loss Account
6 months July–December 1992

	£	£
Sales 13,900 × £6	83,400	
11,800 × £8	94,400	
		177,800
Less Cost of sales		
Opening stock	25,000	
Purchase	86,000	
Closing stock	(38,000)	
		73,000
Gross profit		104,800
Less expenses		
Wages and salaries	62,000	
Overheads	45,000	
Depreciation (6 months)	8,500	
		(115,500)
Net loss		(10,700)

(iii)

Freewheel Ltd
Budgeted Balance Sheet
As at 31 December 1992

	Cost £	Deprec. Prov. £	NBV £
Fixed assets	170,000	22,500	147,500
Current assets			
Stock	38,000		
Trade Debtors	27,200		
Bank		65,200	
Creditors: Amounts falling due within one year:			
Trade creditors	24,000		
Other creditors	41,000		
Bank overdraft	3,800		
		(68,800)	
Net current assets			(3,600)
Total assets less current liabilities			143,900
Shares			120,000
Profit and loss account			23,900
			143,900

(b) The answer should draw attention to:
  (i) The net loss for the year.
  (ii) The overdraft at the end of the period and the fact that dividends and asset payments are due shortly mean that there is an urgent need to arrange overdraft cover.
  (iii) Stocks have increased from two months to three months purchases even though sales have declined. Why has this occurred?
  (iv) Sales have declined in November and December. The reasons for the decline should be investigated.

Answer to question 13.9

(a)

	June £	July £	August £
Closing stock	3,500	6,000	4,000
Material usage	8,000	9,000	10,000
	11,500	15,000	14,000
Less: Opening stock	5,000	3,500	6,000
Direct material purchases	6,500	11,500	8,000

(b) *Cash budgets for June, July and August:*

	June £	July £	August £
Receipts			
Sales cash (10%)	4,500	5,000	6,000
credit	29,500	40,500	45,000
	34,000	45,500	51,000
Payments			
Wages	12,000	13,000	14,500
Overheads (less depreciation)	6,500	7,000	8,000
Direct materials	6,500	11,500	8,000
Taxation	–	25,000	–
	25,000	56,500	30,500
Opening balance	11,750	20,750	9,750
Receipts	34,000	45,500	51,000
Payments	25,000	56,500	30,500
Closing balance	20,750	9,750	30,250

(c) See the section on cash budgets in Chapter 13 for the answer to this question.

Answer to question 13.11

(a) *Monthly cash budget:*

	Month 1 £000	Month 2 £000	Month 3 £000	Month 4 £000
Cash inflows:				
Sales (*W1*)	24.0	93.6	92.6	90.7

Cash outflows:

Business purchase	315.0	–	–	–
Delivery van	–	15.0	–	–
Raw materials (*W2*)	–	44.375	29.375	30.625
Direct labour (*W2*)	27.0	17.25	18.0	18.75
Production overhead (*W3*)	10.5	10.5	10.5	10.5
Selling and administration overhead (*W4*)	39.875	14.875	14.875	14.875
	392.375	102.0	72.75	74.75
Surplus/(deficit) for month	(368.375)	(8.4)	19.85	15.95
Opening balance	–	(368.375)	(376.775)	(356.925)
Closing balance	(368.375)	(376.775)	(356.925)	(340.975)

Workings:	Month 1	Month 2	Month 3	Month 4
(*W1*) Cash inflow from sales	24	24	23	24
Cash inflow from credit sales	–	72	72	69
Less discount	–	(2.4)	(2.4)	(2.3)
		69.6	69.6	66.7
Total cash inflow	24	93.6	92.6	90.7

(*W2*) Selling price at a mark-up of 60% on production cost is £8 per unit (£5.00 × 1.60).

Sales units = sales revenue/8.

(000 units)	Month 1	Month 2	Month 3	Month 4	Month 5	Month 6
Sales	12	12	11.5	12	12.5	13
+ Closing stock of finished goods	12	11.5	12	12.5	13	
− Opening stock of finished goods	6	12	11.5	12	12.5	
= Production	18	11.5	12	12.5	13	
+ Closing stock of raw materials	5.75	6	6.25	6.5		
− Opening stock of raw materials	6	5.75	6	6.25		
= Purchase of raw materials	17.75	11.75	12.25	12.75		

Raw material cost (£000)	Month 1	Month 2	Month 3	Month 4
= Purchases at £2.50	44.375	29.375	30.265	31.875
Raw material payment (£000)	–	44.375	29.375	30.625
Direct labour cost and payment (£000)				
= Production × £1.50	27	17.25	18	18.75

(*W3*) Production overhead = £1.00 × 150,000 units

	= £150,000
Less depreciation	£24,000 (£120,000/5)
Annual payment	£126,000
Monthly payment	£10,500

(*W4*) Selling and administration overhead = £208,000

Less depreciation (year 1)	4,500 (£15,000 × 30%)
	203,500
Less rent and rates	25,000
Year 1 payment	178,500 (excluding rent and rates)
Monthly payment	£14,875 (plus £25,000 in month 1)

(b)

	£
Finished goods stock (12,500 units × £5 per unit)	62,500
Raw materials stock (6,500 units × £2.50 per unit)	16,250
Debtors	69,600
	148,350
Creditors	31,875

Apart from the purchase of the business, the cash budget suggests that there will be sufficient cash inflows to meet the cash outflows. The current assets and debtors provide sufficient funds to cover the creditors. However, this does not take into account possible funding by bank overdraft to finance the business purchase.

Answer to question 13.12

(a) (i) *Cash budget:*

	January £	February £	March £	April £
Balance b/d	10,000	9,000	3,890	9,090
Sales (*W1*)	–	15,200	57,100	80,000
	10,000	24,200	60,990	89,090
Purchases (*W3*)	–	11,550	24,500	26,950
Wages (*W4*)	–	4,800	19,800	22,200
Variable overhead (*W5*)	–	960	4,600	7,080
Fixed overhead (*W6*)	1,000	3,000	3,000	3,000
	1,000	20,310	51,900	59,230
Balance c/d	9,000	3,890	9,090	29,860

Workings:
(*W1*) Sales

	Amount	20%	Discount 5%	Net	50%	20%	8%	Total cash receipts
January	–	–	–	–	–	–	–	
February	80,000	16,000	800	15,200				15,200
March	90,000	18,000	900	17,100	40,000			57,100
April	100,000	20,000	1,000	19,000	45,000	16,000		80,000
May	100,000	20,000	1,000	19,000	50,000	18,000	6,400	93,400

(*W2*) Production:

					Total
January	800				800
February	2,400	900			3,300
March		2,700	1,000		3,700
April			3,000	1,000	4,000
May				3,000	
	3,200	3,600	4,000	4,000	

(W3) Purchases at £7 per unit:

	Production	Current month	Following month	Total	Value (£)
January	February (3,300)		1,650	1,650	11,550
February	March (3,700)	1,650	1,850	3,500	24,500
March	April (4,000)	1,850	2,000	3,850	26,950

(W4) Direct wages:

February payment	800 × £6 =	£4,800
March payment	3,300 × £6 =	£19,800
April payment	3,700 × £6 =	£22,200

(W5) Variable overhead at £2 per unit:

Production	February £	March £	April £	May £
January (£1,600)	960	640		
February (£6,600)		3,960	2,640	
March (£7,400)			4,440	2,960
	960	4,600	7,080	2,960

(W6) Fixed overhead:

	January £	February £	March £	April £
January	1,000	2,000		
February		1,000	2,000	
March			1,000	2,000
April				1,000
	1,000	3,000	3,000	3,000

(ii) It is assumed that the question relates to the amount received from customers in May and not the amount due. The answer is £93,400 (see W1).

(b) A software package would eliminate the tedious arithmetical calculations that are necessary to produce cash budgets. Furthermore, it would enable alternative scenarios to be considered such as what the outcome would be if any of the parameters were changed

Answer to question 13.17

(a) *JK Limited production budget:*

	J	K
Required by sales	10,000	6,000
Closing stock	510	680
	10,510	6,680
Opening stock	(600)	(800)
	9,910	5,880

(b) *Raw materials purchases budget:*

	X		Y	
Required by production:				
J	99,100	(9,910 × 10)	39,640	(9,910 × 4)
K	35,280	(5,880 × 6)	47,040	(5,880 × 8)
	134,380		86,680	
Closing stock	340		170	
	134,720		86,850	
Opening stock	(400)		(200)	
Purchase quantity	134,320		86,650	
Purchase price	£1.50		£4.00	
Purchase cost	£201,480		£346,600	

(c) *Production cost budget:*

	£	£
Opening stock of materials (£480 + £600)		1,080
Purchase of materials		548,080
		549,160
Closing stock of materials (£510 + £680)		(1,190)
		547,970
Direct labour:		
J	9,910 × 6 hrs × £6= 356,760	
K	5,880 × 4 hrs × £6= 141,120	497,880
Variable overhead:		
J	9,910 × 6 hrs × £2= 118,920	
K	5,880 × 4 hrs × £2= 47,040	165,960
Fixed overhead		315,900
		£1,527,710

(d) *Budgeted trading account:*

		£	£
Sales J (10,000 × £135)		1,350,000	
K (6,000 × £145)		870,000	2,220,000
Opening stocks: J		42,000	
K		48,000	
		90 000	
Production costs		1,527,710	
		1,617,710	
Closing stocks: J	51,918[a]		
K	59,976[a]	(111,894)	
			(1,505,816)
Gross profit			714,184)

Notes:
[a] Value of finished goods closing stocks:

	J		K	
Material X	15	(10 × £1.50)	9	(6 × £1.50)
Material Y	16	(4 × £4)	32	(8 × £4)
Direct labour	36		24	
Variable overhead	12		8	
Fixed overhead[b]	22.80		15.20	
	£101.80		£88.20	
Closing stock (units)	510		680	
	£51,918		£59,976	

[b] Fixed overhead rate per hour:

$$\frac{£315,900 \text{ fixed overheads}}{(9,910 \times 6 \text{ hrs}) + (5,880 \times 4 \text{ hrs})} = £3.80 \text{ per hour}$$

Answer to question 13.19

(a)

Product		A		B		C	Total
Sales mix weighting		1		2		4	
		£		£		£	£
Unit selling price		215		250		300	
Unit costs:							
Frame		20		20		20	
Component D (at £8 per unit)	40		8		24		
F (at £5 per unit)	5		35		25		
F (at £3 per unit)	12	57	15	58	3	52	
Labour:							
Skilled (at £6 per hour)	12		9		9		
Unskilled (at £4.50 per hour)	9	21	9	18	13.5	22.5	
Variable production overhead		5		4		3.5	
Contribution		112		150		202	
Weighted by sales mix		112		300		808	1,220
Required period 1 contribution:				£m			
Profit		0.500 (£6.5 m/13)					
Add fixed costs:							
Production		0.056 (£0.728 m/13)					
Selling and distribution		0.028 (£0.364 m/13)					
Administration		0.026 (£0.338 m/13)					
		0.610					

∴ 500 (£610,000/£1,220) 'mixes' must be sold each period.

(i) *Sales budget:*

	A	B	C
Sales quantities	500	1,000	2,000
Sales value (£)	107,500	250,000	600,000

(ii) *Production budget:*

Sales quantities	500	1,000	2,000
Closing stock	270	630	1,440
	770	1,630	3,440
Opening stock	300	700	1,600
Production	470	930	1,840

(iii) *Material usage budget:*

Usage:				Total (units)
Frame	470	930	1,840	3,240
D	2,350	930	5,520	8,800
E	470	6,510	9,200	16,180
F	1,880	4,650	1,840	8,370

(iv) *Purchases budget:*

Purchases (units):	Frame	D	E	F
Closing stock	900	3,600	9,000	3,600
Add used in production	3,240	8,800	16,180	8,370
	4,140	12,400	25,180	11,970
Less opening stock	1,000	4,000	10,000	4,000
Purchases (units)	3,140	8,400	15,180	7,970
Cost (£)	62,800	67,200	75,900	23,910

(v) *Manpower budgets:*

	Machining (hours)	Assembly (hours)
A (units produced × hrs per unit)	940	940
B	1,395	1,860
C	2,760	5,520
	5,095	8,320
Hours available per period (4 × 37.5)	150	150
Number of people required	34	56

(b) The following factors would need to be considered:

(i) The ability to be able to plan future production requirements, since production might be halted if there was a sudden increase in production. If production is volatile, there is a danger that stockouts might occur.

(ii) The speed and reliability of the delivery service. If suppliers can deliver at short notice then stockouts are less likely to occur.

(iii) The extra costs involved arising from more frequent deliveries in terms of ordering costs and quantity discounts.

(iv) Alterative use of storage space.

(v) The savings in holding costs arising from the reduction in stocks. Stock reductions in units would be as follows:

	Frames	D	E	F
End of period 1	900	3,600	9,000	3,600
Requirements for 1 week	810 (3,240/4)	2,200 (8,800/4)	4,045 (16,180/4)	2,092 (8,370/4)
Stock reduction	90	1,400	4,955	1,508

Answer to question 13.20

(a)		Product Y £	Product Z £
	Current standards:		
	Direct materials:		
	A: 30 kg at £5.20 per kg	156.00	
	15 kg at £5.20 per kg		78.00
	B: 30 kg at £1.80 per kg	54.00	
	40 kg at £1.80 per kg		72.00
	Direct labour:		
	Mixing (2.5 hours at £4.50)	11.25	11.25
	Packaging (5 hours at £4)	20.00	20.00
	New standards:		
	Direct materials:		
	A: 29.333 kg^a at £5.46 per kg	160.16	
	14.667 kg^b at £5.46 per kg		80.08
	B: 30 kg at £1.89 per kg	56.70	
	40 kg at £1.89 per kg		75.60
	Direct labour:		
	Mixing (2.5 hours at £4.86)	12.15	12.15
	Packaging (5 hours at £4.32)	21.60	21.60

Notes:
^{a} Input for material A excluding loss = 26.667 kg (30/1.125)
　Revised input for material A　　= 29.333 kg (26.66 × 1.10)
^{b} Input excluding loss　　　　　= 13.333 kg (15/1.125)
　Revised input　　　　　　　　= 14.667 kg (13.333 kg × 1.10)

(b)　(i)　*Production budget:*

	Product Y (units)	Product Z (units)
Sales	1,700,000	950,000
Add closing stock	200,000	125,000
	1,900,000	1,075,000
Less opening stock	190,000	150,000
Production	1,710,000	925,000

(ii)　*Material B purchases budget:*

	kg
Required for production:	
Product Y:	
1,710,000 units at 30 kg per hundred	513,000
Product Z:	
925,000 units at 40 kg per hundred	370,000
	883,000
Add closing stock	90,000
	973,000
Less opening stock	95,000
Purchases	878,000

(iii) *Mixing labour budget:*
Total production:

Product Y	1,710,000
Product Z	925,000
	2,635,000 units

at 2.5 hours per hundred
= 65,875 hours

(c) For the answer to this question you should refer to the section on why do we produce budgets in Chapter 13. In particular, the answer should describe planning, coordinating, communicating, motivating, control and evaluation roles of budgets.

Answer to question 13.24

Task 1

Alderley Ltd Budget Statements 13 weeks to 4 April 1997

(a) Production Budget

	Elgar units	Hoist units
Budgeted sales volume	845	1,235
Add closing stock[a]	78	266
Less Opening stock	(163)	(361)
Units of production	760	1,140

(b) Material Purchases Budget

	Elgar kg	Hoist kg	Total kg
Material consumed	5,320(760 × 7)	9,120(1,140 × 8)	14,440
Add raw material closing stock[b]			2,888
Less raw material opening stock			(2,328)
Purchases (kg)			15,000

(c) Purchases (£) (1,500 × £12)   £180,000

(d) Production Labour Budget

	Elgar hours	Hoist hours	Total hours
Standard hours produced[c]	6,080	5,700	11,780
Productivity adjustment (5/95 × 11,780)			620
Total hours employed			12,400
Normal hours employed[d]			11,544
Overtime hours			856

(e) Labour cost   £
Normal hours (11,544 × £8)   92,352
Overtime (856 × £8 × 125%)   8,560
Total   100,912

Notes:
[a] Number of days per period = 13 weeks × 5 days = 65
Stock: Elgar = (6/65) × 845 = 78, Holst = (14/65) × 1,235 = 266
[b] (13/65) × (5,320 + 9,120) = 2,888

^{c} Elgar 760 $\times$ 8 hours = 6,080, Holst 1,140 $\times$ 5 hours = 5,700
^{d} 24 employees $\times$ 37 hours $\times$ 13 weeks = 11,544

Task 2

(a) Four ways of forecasting future sales volume are:

(i) Where the number of customers is small it is possible to interview them to ascertain what their likely demand will be over the forecasting period.

(ii) Produce estimates based on the opinion of executives and sales personnel. For example, sales personnel may be asked to estimate the sales of each product to their customers, or regional sales managers may estimate the total sales for each of their regions.

(iii) Market research may be necessary where it is intended to develop new products or new markets. This may involve interviews with existing and potential customers in order to estimate potential demand.

(iv) Estimates involving statistical techniques that incorporate general business and market conditions and past growth in sales.

(b) Interviewing customers and basing estimates on the opinions of sales personnel are likely to be more appropriate for existing products and customers involving repeat sales. Market research is appropriate for new products or markets and where the market is large and anticipated revenues are likely to be sufficient to justify the cost of undertaking the research.

Statistical estimates derived from past data are likely to be appropriate where conditions are likely to be stable and past demand patterns are likely to be repeated through time. This method is most suited to existing products or markets where sufficient data is available to establish a trend in demand.

(c) The major limitation of interviewing customers is that they may not be prepared to divulge the information if their future plans are commercially sensitive. There is also no guarantee that the orders will be placed with Alderley Ltd. They may place their orders with competitors.

Where estimates are derived from sales personnel there is a danger that they might produce over-optimistic estimates in order to obtain a favourable performance rating. Alternatively, if their future performance is judged by their ability to achieve the budgeted sales they may be motivated to under-estimate sales demand.

Market research is expensive and may produce unreliable estimates if inexperienced researchers are used. Also small samples are often used which may not be indicative of the population and this can result in inaccurate estimates.

Statistical estimates will produce poor demand estimates where insufficient past data is available, demand is unstable over time and the future environment is likely to be significantly different from the past. Statistical estimates are likely to be inappropriate for new products and new markets where past data is unavailable.

Answer to question 13.25

(a) Let t be the month for which forecast is required, so that:

t_0 = current month

t_1 = next month
t_{-1} = previous month
Let S be the sales for the current month.
The equations for use in the cash budgeting model are as follows:

$$\text{sales} = S(1.01)^t$$

Cost of sales = $0.75S$ (gross profit margin is $33\frac{1}{3}\%$ on cost of sales: therefore cost of sales is 75% of sales)
Cash collections t months from now:

$$0.2S(1.01)^t + 0.8[0.2S(1.01)^{t-1}] + 0.8[0.6S(1.01)^{t-2}] + 0.8[0.2S(1.01)^{t-3}]$$

Purchases t months from now:

$$0.75S(1.01)^{t+2}$$

Payments for purchases t months from now:

$$0.75S(1.01)^{t+1}$$

Payment for expenses t months from now:

$$0.05S(1.01)^{t-1} + 3,000 + 10,000$$

(b) S for June = £100,000

$t = 3$ (month of September is $t + 3$ months from June)

Collections during September:

$$0.2S(1.01)^t + 0.8[0.2S(1.01)^{t-1}] + 0.8[0.6S(1.01)^{t-2}] + 0.8[0.2S(1.01)^{t-3}]$$
$$= 0.2(100,000)(1.01)^3 + 0.8(0.2)(100,000)(1.01)^2 + 0.8(0.6)(100,000)(1.01)$$
$$+ 0.8(0.2)(100,000)$$
$$= £20,606 + £16,322 + £48,480 + £16,000$$
$$= £101,408$$

Payments for purchases during September:

$$0.75S(1.01)^{t+1} = 0.75(100,000)(1.01)^4 = £78,045$$

Payments for expenses during September:

$$= 0.05S(1.01)^2 + 3,000 + 10,000$$
$$= £5,100 + £3,000 + £10,000 = £18,100$$

The cash flow statement for September is as follows:

	£	£
Receipts from sales		101,408
Payments; Purchases	78,045	
Payroll	5,100	
Utilities	3,000	
Other costs	10,000	96,145
Increase in cash		5,263

(c) The following procedures can be applied to incorporate uncertainty:
  (i)   Sensitivity analysis
  (ii) Expected values
  (iii) Simulation

The simplest approach for cash budgeting is to apply sensitivity analysis. By asking 'What if?' questions, such as changes in percentages for cash received each month from debtors, or changes in sales growth, the variability of possible outcomes can be ascertained.

Control in the organization

Answers to Chapter 14

Question summary

14.1 to 14.3
Various discussion questions relevant to Chapter 14.

14.4 and 14.5
Preparation of cash and flexible budgets.

14.6 to 14.8
Preparation of flexible budgets. Question 14.6 requires the calculation of fixed and variable costs and 14.7 requires the application of a budget formula to determine the flexible budget allowance. Question 14.8 also requires a discussion of the motivation role of budgets.

14.9
Criticisms and redrafting of a monthly performance report.

14.10 to 14.14
Questions relating to flexible budgeting. Question 14.10 also involves the preparation of sales budgets based on limiting factors. Questions 14.11 and 14.12 require comments and explanations of the variances. Question 14.14 requires the preparation of a performance report adopting a flexible budgeting approach.

14.15
Comments on budget preparation and suggestions for improving the performance reports.

14.16
Sales forecasting, removing seasonal variations, flexible budgets and budget preparation.

Answer to question 14.5

(a)

Activity level (%)	90%	100%	110%	120%
Activity level (direct labour hours – DLHs)	108,000	120,000	132,000	144,000
Fixed costs:	£	£	£	£
Depreciation	22,000	22,000	22,000	22,000
Staff salaries	43,000	43,000	43,000	43,000
Insurances	9,000	9,000	9,000	9,000
Rent and rates	12,000	12,000	12,000	12,000
Variable costs:				
Power	32,400	36,000	39,600	43,200
Consumables	5,400	6,000	6,600	7,200
Direct labour	378,000	420,000	462,000	504,000
Semi-variable costs:[a]				
Fixed element	55,000	55,000	55,000	55,000
Variable element	270,00	300,000	330,000	360,000
Total	826,800	903,000	979,200	1,055,400

Note:

[a] The separation of costs into the fixed and variable elements is calculated from past data using the high/low method:

	DLHs	Total cost £
High (1988)	110,000	330,000
Low (1983)	80,000	255,000
Increase	30,000	75,000

Variable cost per DLH = £2.50 (£75,000/30,000 DLHs)
Fixed cost = £55,000 [£330,000 − (110,000 × £2.50)]

(b)   (i) *Cash budget:*

	January	February	March	April	May	June
Cash balance	2,000	(4,500)	(3,200)	(3,800)	2,300	9,800
+ Cash from sales	18,000	19,000	22,000	24,000	25,000	29,000
	20,000	14,500	18,800	20,200	27,300	38,800
− Cash payments						
Materials	9,000	10,000	7,000	9,000	11,000	4,000
Labour	3,900	4,000	4,200	4,700	3,700	4,100
Overhead	3,600	3,700	3,900	4,200	2,800	3,500
Capital			7,500			27,200
Tax	8,000					
	24,500	17,700	22,600	17,900	17,500	38,800

(ii) The firm should take the following action:

(1) It should arrange appropriate overdraft facilities from February to April.

(2) The company pays suppliers one month after delivery but allows customers two months' credit. The company should consider delaying payment to suppliers by an extra month.

(3) There is a zero cash balance at the *end* of June and this suggests the possibility of future liquidity problems.

Answer to question 14.6

(a) *Workings:*

Volume of activity at 100% level = 50,000 units (£1.5 m/£30)

The variable cost per unit is calculated from the following formula:

$$\frac{\text{Change in costs}}{\text{Change in activity}}$$

	£
Material cost	7.50 (£37,000/5,000 units)
Labour costs	9.00 (£45,000/5,000 units)
Production overhead	3.50 (£17,500/5,000 units)
Administration	2.00 (£10,000/5,000 units)
Selling and distribution	1.00 (£5,000/5,000 units)
	23.00

Fixed costs are calculated by deducting total variable costs from total costs. The calculations (at 100% activity) are as follows:

	£
Materials	Nil
Labour	35,000 (£485.000 − £450.000)
Production overhead	60,000 (£235,000 − £1175.00)
Administration	30,000 (£130.000 − £100.000)
Selling and distribution	25,000 (£75.000 − £50.000)
	150,000

	Flexed budget at 75% activity (37,500 units)	Actual	Variances Favourable (Adverse)	
	£	£	£	£
Revenue	1,125,000	1,075,000		(50,000)
Less costs				
Material costs	281,250	311,750	(30,500)	
Labour costs	372,500	351,500	21,000	
Production costs	191,250	171,250	20,000	
Administration costs	105,000	117,500	(12,500)	
Selling and distribution	62,500	66,500	(4,000)	
	1,012.500	1,018,500		(6,000)
Profit	112,500	56,500		(56,000)

(b) The actual profit is £56,000 less than budgeted profit for the actual level of activity. There is an adverse sales variance of £50,000 due to a reduction in the selling price. The sales variance accounts for most of the profit variance. The reason for the selling price reduction should be investigated. Was the reduction due to the depressed state of the market or an attempt to generate increased sales revenue in order to increase market share? The pricing policy should be investigated.

The labour cost and production variances are favourable possibly due to an increase in efficiency, cost reduction and a reduction in overtime. There was an adverse material variance of £30,500. This needs to be investigated. Possible reasons for the variance include the purchase of higher quality materials than planned. excessive wastage due to new production methods or the use of new untrained or unskilled workers. The latter may have resulted in the favourable labour wage rate variances.

All the variances should be investigated and appropriate remedial action taken.

(c) It is assumed that the change in the cost structure refers only to the order for 12,500 units (50,000 units − 37,500 units). The relevant revenues and costs are as follows:

	£
Selling price per unit	25.00
Materials	(7.50)
Labour (£9 + £1)	(10.00)
Production (£3.50 × 1.20)	(4.20)
Administration (£2 × 1.25)	(2.50)
Selling and distribution	(1.00)
Contribution	(0.20)

Contribution for 12,500 units (£2,500)

The order should be rejected because it provides a negative contribution of £2,500.

Answer to question 14.7

(a) The question only provides a partial cost analysis. To ascertain the cost formula for each item of expense it is necessary to ascertain the missing information for the activity level given in the question (2,000 ORN and 4,300V):

Item of expense	Budgeted expenditure	Variable cost		Fixed cost
	£		£	£
Cleaning	13,250	2,000 × £2.50	= 5,000	8,250
Laundry	15,025	4,300 × £1.75	= 7,525	7,500
Reception	13,100	£1,000/2,000 × 2,000	= 1,000	12,100
Maintenance	11,100	2,000 × £0.80	= 1,600	9,500
Housekeeping	19,600	£8,600/4,300 × 4,300	= 8,600	11,000
Administration	7,700	2,000 × £0.20	= 400	7,300
Catering	21,460	4,300 × £2.20	= 9,460	12,000
General overheads	11,250		= 0	11,250

Note that the variable cost or the fixed cost is the balancing figure in the above calculations. We can now compute the flexible budget for period 9.

Flexible budget for period 9 (Activity = 1,850 ORN and 4,575V):

	Variable cost		Fixed cost	Total cost
		£	£	£
Cleaning	1,850 × £2.50 =	4,625	8,250	12,875
Laundry	4,575 × £1.75 =	8,006	7,500	15,506
Reception	1,850 × £0.50 =	925	12,100	13,025
Maintenance	1,850 × £0.80 =	1,480	9,500	10,980
Housekeeping	4,575 × £2 =	9,150	11,000	20,150
Administration	1,850 × £0.20 =	370	7,300	7,670
Catering	4,575 × £2.20 =	10,065	12,000	22,065
General overheads	=	0	11,250	11,250
				113,521

(b)

	Flexed budget	Actual	Variance	Favourable/ adverse
	£	£	£	
Cleaning	12,875	13,292	(417)	ADV
Laundry	15,506	14,574	932	FAV
Reception	13,025	13,855	(830)	ADV
Maintenance	10,980	10,462	518	FAV
Housekeeping	20,150	19,580	570	FAV
Administration	7,670	7,930	(260)	ADV
Catering	22,065	23,053	(988)	ADV
General overheads	11,250	11,325	(75)	ADV
	113,521	114,071	(550)	

(c) See the section on why do we produce budgets in Chapter 13 for the answer to this question.

Answer to question 14.10

(a) See the section on determining the factor which restricts performance and preparation of the sales budget for the answer to this question. In particular the answer should stress that the principal budget factor is the factor which determines the level of activity. This will normally be the level of sales but it could also be any resource in the business which restricts the volume of sales (for example, machine capacity, labour or shortage of materials). The principal budget factor is therefore important because it determines the level of activity on which all budgets will be based.

(b) A fixed budget is a budget which remains unchanged irrespective of the volume of activity whereas a flexible budget is adjusted to the level of activity which is actually attained. See the section on flexible budgeting in Chapter 14 for a description of flexible budgeting.

   Flexed budgets should be used for control purposes: costs should be controlled by comparing actual costs with the actual level of activity and not some level of activity which was assumed when the budget was prepared. Fixed budgets are appropriate for planning purposes for determining the planned level of activity, but for control purposes actual expenses should he compared with an adjusted budget based on the actual level of activity.

(c) (i) *The direct labour hours required for the first sales forecast are:*

	Product A	Product B	Product C	Total
First sales forecast	£44,000	£60,000	£6,000	£110,000
Second sales forecast	£60,000	£75,000	£7,000	£142,000

The principal budget factors are:

First sales forecast = Sales
Second sales forecast = Direct labour

(ii) *Sales limitation (first forecast):*

	A	B	C	Total
Sales volume	22,000	40,000	6,000	
Contribution per unit	£4	£2	£2	
Total contribution	£88,000	£80,000	£12,000	£180,000
		Less fixed costs		£150,000
		Profit		£30,000

Direct labour limiting factor (second sales forecast):

	A	B	C
(1) Contribution per unit	£3	£1.70	£1.60
(2) Contribution per £1 of labour	£1.50 (£3/2)	£1.13 (£1.70/1.50)	£1.60 (£1.60/1)
(3) Ranking	2	3	1
(4) Sales allocation (Note)	30,000	45,333	7,000
(5) Contribution (1) × (4)	£90,000	£77,066	£11,200

	£
Total contribution	178,266
Fixed costs	150,000
Profit	28,266

Note:
The sales allocation is calculated as follows:

	Sales volume	Direct labour cost	Balance of direct labour cost available
Product C	7,000	£7,000	£128,000
Product A	30,000	£60,000	£68,000
Product B	45,333 (£68,000/£1.50)	£68,000	–

Answer to question 14.12

(a) *Flexible budget at 85% activity:*

	£	£
Variable cost		
Direct materials[a]	1,386,056	
Direct wages[b]	2,356,949	
Variable production overhead[c]	489,584	
Variable selling and distribution overhead[d]	69,940	
		4,302,529
Fixed costs		
Fixed production overhead[c]	330,115	
Fixed selling and distribution overhead[d]	161,266	
Administration overhead	132,000	623,381
Total cost		4,925,910
Sales[e]		5,911,092
Profit		985,182

Notes:
[a] Costs increase by £153,800 for each of the changes in activity. Thus at 85% capacity level costs will be (£1,153,800 + £153,800) 1.04 after taking account of the predicted price change of 4%.

[b] Costs have increased by increments of £269,150. At 85% capacity level predicted costs are (£2,019,150 + £269,150) 1.03.

[c] Costs have increased by increments of £53,830. However, the question indicates that there is a fixed and variable element. Therefore at 85% capacity variable costs are predicted to be 8.5 (10% increments) × £53,830 per 10% increment = £457,555 × 1.07 price increase = £489,584. The fixed cost element before the price increase is £703,830 total costs at 75% capacity less variable costs of 7.5 (10% increments) × £53,830 = £300,105. The predicted fixed costs after the price increase are £300,105 (1.10) = £330,115.

[d] Costs have increased in increments of £7,690. Using the same principles as those outlined in [c] variable costs at 85% capacity are predicted to be 8.5 × £7,690(1.07 inflation factor) = £69,940. Fixed cost element = £207,690 total cost at 75% capacity less 7.5 (£7,690) = £150,015 before the price increase. After the price increase the estimated fixed costs will be £150,015(1.075) = £161,266.

[e] Total cost (£4,925,910) × 100/83.333.

(b) Problems that can arise from a change in capacity level include:
1. Step increase in fixed costs to enable output to be expanded (see the section on changes in fixed costs and selling prices in Chapter 9).
2. Inability to sell the increased output resulting in an increase in stocks.
3. Working the plant more intensively might result in bottlenecks and machine breakdowns and this may result in an increase in unit variable costs because of diminishing returns to scale (see the section on the economist's model in Chapter 9).

(c) The budget committee should consist of high-level executives who represent the major segments of the business. For example, the committee might consist of the chief executive (or his or her deputy), the production manager, the marketing manager, the management accountant and the human resource manager. Its major task is to communicate the long-term objectives of the organization, ensure that the budgets are realistically established and that they are coordinated satisfactorily.

Answer to question 14.14

Task 1
Reclamation Division Performance Report – 4 weeks to 31 May 1997:
Original budget   250 tonnes
Actual output   200 tonnes

	Budget based on 200 tonnes	Actual	Variance	Comments
Controllable expenses:				
Wages and social security costs[a]	43,936	46,133	2,197A	
Fuel[b]	15,000	15,500	500A	
Consumables[c]	2,000	2,100	100A	
Power[d]	1,500	1,590	90A	
Directly attributable overheads[e]	20,000	21,000	1,000A	
	82,436	86,323	3,887A	
Non-controllable expenses:				
Plant maintenance[e]	5,950	6,900	950A	
Central services[e]	6,850	7,300	450A	
	12,800	14,200	1,400A	
Total	95,236	100,523	5,287A	

Notes:
[a] 6 employees × 4 teams × 42 hours per week × £7.50 per hour × 4 weeks = £30,240.
[b] 200 tonnes × £75
[c] 200 tonnes × £10
[d] £500 + (£5 × 200) = £1,500
[e] It is assumed that directly attributable expenses, plant maintenance and central services are non-variable expenses.

Task 2
(a) (i) Past knowledge can provide useful information on future outcomes but ideally budgets ought to be based on the most up-to-date information. Budgeting should be related to the current environment and the use of past information that is two years old can only be justified where the operating conditions and environment are expected to remain unchanged.
    (ii) For motivation and planning purposes budgets should represent targets based on what we are proposing to do. For control purposes budgets should be flexed based on what was actually done so that actual costs for actual output can be compared with budgeted costs for the actual output. This ensures that valid comparisons will be made.
    (iii) For variable expenses the original budget should be reduced in proportion to reduced output in order to reflect cost behaviour. Fixed costs are not adjusted since they are unaffected in the short-term by output

changes. Flexible budgeting ensures that like is being compared with like so that reduced output does not increase the probability that favourable cost variances will be reported. However, if less was produced because of actual sales being less than budget this will result in an adverse sales variance and possibly an adverse profit variance.

(iv) Plant maintenance costs are apportioned on the basis of capital values and therefore newer equipment (with higher written-down values) will be charged with a higher maintenance cost. Such an approach does not provide a meaningful estimate of maintenance resources consumed by departments since older equipment is likely to be more expensive to maintain. The method of recharging should be reviewed and ideally based on estimated usage according to maintenance records. The charging of the overspending by the maintenance department to user departments is questionable since this masks inefficiencies. Ideally, maintenance department costs should be recharged based on actual usage at budgeted cost and the maintenance department made accountable for the adverse spending (price) variance.

(v) The comments do not explain the causes of the variances and are presented in a negative tone. No comments are made, nor is any praise given, for the favourable variances.

(vi) Not all variances should be investigated. The decision to investigate should depend on both their absolute and relative size and the likely benefits arising from an investigation.

(vii) Central service costs are not controllable by divisional managers. However, even though the divisional manager cannot control these costs there is an argument for including them as non-controllable costs in the performance report. The justification for this is that divisional managers are made aware of central service costs and may put pressure on central service staff to control such costs more effectively. It should be made clear to divisional managers that they are not accountable for any non-controllable expenses that are included in their performance reports.

Answer to question 14.16

Task 1

(a)

	Quarter 1 units	Quarter 2 units	Quarter 3 units	Quarter 4 units
Actual sales volume	420,000	450,000	475,000	475,000
Seasonal variation	+25,000	+15,000	–	−40,000
Deseasonalized sales volumes	395,000	435,000	475,000	515,000

(b) The trend is for sales volume to increase by 40,000 units each quarter:

Forecast for next year	Quarter 1 units	Quarter 2 units	Quarter 3 units	Quarter 4 units
Trend projection	555,000	595,000	635,000	675,000
Seasonal variation	+25,000	+15,000	–	−40,000
Forecast sales volumes	580,000	610,000	635,000	635,000

Task 2

(a) Seasonal variations represent consistent patterns in sales volume that occur throughout each year. For example, the seasonal variation of +25,000 for Quarter 1 indicates that sales volume in the first quarter tends to be 25,000 units higher than the underlying trend in sales. In contrast, the seasonal variation of −40,000 in Quarter 4 indicates that sales in this quarter tend to be 40,000 units lower than the underlying trend in sales.

  To derive the deseasonalized data the seasonal variations must be removed so that a trend can be observed. The above figures indicate an increase of 40,000 units per quarter. This trend is concealed when the actual data is observed because of the distorting effects of seasonal variations. Observations of the actual data suggests that the rate of increase in sales is declining.

(b) Provided that the observed trend in deseasonalized data continues the deseasonalized data can be used to project the trend in future sales. The trend values are adjusted by seasonal variations in each quarter to predict actual sales.

Task 3

(a) A fixed budget is a budget for the planned level of activity and budgeted costs are not adjusted to the actual level of activity. A fixed budget is used at the planning stage because an activity level has to be initially determined so that all department activities can be coordinated to meet the planned level of activity. However, it is most unlikely that actual activity will be the same as the planned level of activity. For example, if the actual level of activity is greater than budgeted level of activity then those costs that vary with the level of activity will be greater than the budgeted costs purely because of changes in activity. It is clearly inappropriate for variable costs to compare actual costs at one level of activity with budgeted costs at another level of activity. The original fixed budget must be adjusted to reflect the budgeted expenditure at the actual level of activity. This procedure is called flexible budgeting. The resulting comparison of actual costs with a flexible budget is more meaningful for cost control because the effect of the change in the activity level has been eliminated.

(b) Possible activity indicators include number of deliveries made, miles travelled and journeys made.

(c) See the section on budget formula in Chapter 14 for the answer to this question.

Task 4

(a) Production budget for product Q

	units
Forecast sales for year	18,135
Increase in stock (15% × 1,200)	180
Finished units required	18,315
Quality control loss (1/99)	185
Total units input to production	18,500

(b) Direct labour budget for product Q

	hours
Active labour hours required (18,500 × 5)	92,500
Idle time allowance (7.5/92.5)	7,500
Total hours to be paid for	100,000
Standard hourly rate	£6
Budgeted labour cost	£600,000

(c) Material usage budget for material M

	kg
Material required for processing	
18,500 units ($\times$ 9 kg)	166,500
Wastage (10/90)	18,500
Material usage for year	185,000

(d) Material purchases budget for material M

	kg
Material required for production input	185,000
Increase in material stocks (12%)	960
Expected loss in stores	1,000
Material purchases required	186,960

Task 5

The implications of the shortage is that the budget plans cannot be achieved and the availability of material is the limiting factor. If the limiting factor cannot be removed the materials purchase budget should be the first budget to be prepared and all the other budgets coordinated to ensure the most efficient usage of materials. The following four possible actions could be taken to overcome the problem:

(i) Seek alternative supplies for material M. Possible problems include the reliability and quality of materials delivered by new suppliers. New suppliers should be carefully vetted prior to entering into any contracts or making company plans dependent on deliveries from new suppliers.

(ii) Reduce the budgeted sales of product Q. This will lead to loss in profits and the possible permanent loss of customers to competitors if the competitors are able to meet customer demand.

(iii) Reduce the stock levels for product Q and material M. The danger with this course of action is that stocks may not be available when required which could lead to disruptions in production and lost sales.

(iv) Reduce the wastage of material M and the defective output of product Q. This course of action will cause problems if quality standards are reduced resulting in inferior quality output. This could have a harmful effect on future sales. Problems will not be caused if quality standards are maintained and improved working practices result in a reduction of waste and defective output.

Standard costing and variance analysis

Answers to Chapter 15

Question summary

15.1 to 15.12
Multiple choice questions.

15.13 and 15.14
Calculation of material and labour variances. Question 15.14 requires the calculation of variances and inputs and outputs from incomplete data.

15.15
Calculation of labour, material and sales variances plus a reconciliation of actual and budgeted profit. Part (b) requires accounting entries for a standard costing system for the purchase and issue of materials.

15.16
Calculation of labour and material variances for a hotel.

15.17 and 15.18
Calculation of labour and material variances and reconciliation of standard and actual cost.

15.19 to 15.25
Calculation of overhead variances. Question 15.20 requires the computation of the budgeted inputs and 15.24 also requires the calculation of labour and material variances.

15.26 to 15.28
Reconciliation of standard and actual costs or budgeted and actual profit involving labour, material and overhead variances.

15.29 to 15.34
Calculation of actual inputs working backwards from reported variances given in the question and the calculation of variances from incomplete information.

15.35
Comparison of standard absorption costing and standard marginal costing.

15.36 to 15.39

Accounting entries for a standard costing system. Question 15.36 requires the preparation of the stores ledger account when the price variance is extracted at the time of issue and also at the time of purchase. Questions 15.37 to 15.39 require the calculation of labour, material and overhead variances. A full absorption costing system is operated with Questions 15.37 and 15.39 whereas 15.38 assumes that a variable costing system is in operation.

Question 15.38 also assumes that the company uses an interlocking accounting system.

15.40 and 15.41

Calculation of productivity ratios. Question 15.40 also involves the calculation of labour and material variances.

Answer to question 15.1

A favourable labour efficiency variance indicates that actual hours used were less than the standard hours produced. The favourable variance was £7,800. Therefore the standard hours produced were 18,700 (17,500 + £7,800/£6.50).

Answer = D

Answer to question 15.2

Materials price variance = (Standard price − Actual price) × Actual quantity
= (Actual quantity × Standard price) − Actual cost
= (8,200 × £0.80) − £6,888
= £328 Adverse

Material usage variance = (Standard quantity − Actual quantity) × Standard price
= (870 × 8 kg = 6,960 − 7,150) × £0.80
= £512 Adverse

Answer = D

Answer to question 15.3

Fixed overhead variance = Budgeted cost (not flexed) − Actual cost
= £10,000 per month − £9,800
= £200 Favourable

Answer = B

Answer to question 15.4

Standard fixed overhead rate = $\dfrac{\text{Budgeted cost (£48,000)}}{\text{Budgeted output (4,800 units)}}$ = £10

Overheads incurred = Budgeted cost + Expenditure variance (£2,000) = £50,000
Overheads absorbed = £50,000 − Under-absorption (£8,000) = £42,000
Actual number of units produced = £42,000/£10 = 4,200

Answer = C

Answer to question 15.5

Volume variance
    = (Actual production − Budgeted production) × Fixed overhead rate
    = (19,500 − 20,000) × (£100,000/20,000)
    = £2,500A

Answer = B

Answer to question 15.6

Sales volume variance = (Actual sales volume − Budgeted sales volume) × Standard contribution margin
= (4,500 − 5,000) £4.40
= £2,200 Adverse

Answer = B

Answer to question 15.7

Standard price per kg = £46,248/11,280 = £4.10
Usage variance (kg) = £492/£4.10 = 120 kg
Actual usage exceeds standard usage by 120 kg
Standard usage = 11,280 − 120 = 11,160 kg

Answer = D

Answer to question 15.8

Budgeted overhead rate = £10 per hour
Actual volume was 1,000 standard hours less than budget thus causing an under-absorption of £10,000. Actual expenditure was £1,400 more than budget thus resulting in an under-absorption of £1,400.

Answer = C

Answer to question 15.9

	£
Actual cost	16,380
Less adverse price variance	1,170
Actual purchases at standard price	15,210

Standard price = £15,210/7,800 kg = £1.95

Answer = A

Answer to question 15.10

Sales volume variance = (Actual sales volume − Budgeted sales volume) × Standard profit margin
= (11,000 − £100,000/£8)£2.50 = £3,750A
Sales price variance = (Actual price − Budgeted price) × Actual sales volume
= (£9 − £8) × 11,000 = £11,000F

Answer = A

Answer to question 15.11

Efficiency variance = (Standard hours − Actual hours) Standard rate
= (4,650 × 4 hrs = 18,600 − 19,100)£5.40
= £2,700A
Rate variance = (Standard rate − Actual rate) Actual hours
= (£5.40 − £98,350/19,100)19,100
= £4,790F

Answer = E

Answer to question 15.12

Efficiency variance = (Standard hours − Actual hours) × Standard rate
= (Standard hours × Standard rate) − (Actual hours − Standard rate)

− £36,000A	= (5,792 × 6.5 hrs × £5 = £188,240) − (AH × £5)
5AH	= £188,240 + £36,000
AH	= 44,848

Answer = D

Answer to question 15.16

Task

(a) Soap pack price variance = (Standard price − Actual price) Actual quantity

$$= (\pounds1.20 - \pounds1.30)\ 920 \quad = \pounds92A$$
$$= (\pounds1.20 - \pounds1.40)\ 1,130 \quad = \underline{\pounds226A}$$
$$\underline{\pounds318A}$$

Soap pack usage variance = (Standard quantity − Actual quantity) Standard price

$$= (8,400 - 8,580)\ \pounds1.20$$
$$= \pounds216A$$

Cleaning labour rate variance = (Standard rate − Actual rate) Actual hours

$$= (\pounds3.60 - \pounds3)\ 1,850 \quad = \pounds1,110F$$
$$= (\pounds3.60 - \pounds4.50)\ 700 \quad = \underline{\pounds630A}$$
$$\underline{\pounds480F}$$

Cleaning labour efficiency
variance = (Standard hours − Actual hours) Standard rate

$$= (8,400 \times 0.25\ \text{hours} = 2,100 - 2,550)\ \pounds3.60$$
$$= \pounds1,620A$$

(b) (i)   The soap price variance could be due to inflation and a general increase in the market price. In such circumstances the standard price should be altered to reflect the current standard price.

(ii) The adverse soap usage variance could be due to theft or excess issues. Managers should check that stocks are securely locked away and that only the standard quantity is issued each day.

(iii) The labour rate variance may have arisen because proportionately less weekend work was undertaken than that allowed for in the standard. It may be appropriate to maintain separate standards for weekend and non-weekend work and separate records so that variances can be reported for both categories of labour.

(iv) The standard time may represent an inappropriate standard that must be changed. Alternatively, excessive idle time may have occurred because of rooms not being vacated when the cleaners are being paid. Working practices and vacation procedures should be investigated to ensure that vacation is synchronized with when the cleaners are employed for cleaning the rooms.

Answer to question 15.17

Task 1

(a) To ascertain the seasonally adjusted price it is necessary to remove the seasonal variations from the observed price:

	Quarter 1	Quarter 2	Quarter 3	Quarter 4
	£	£	£	£
Actual price	10	11	16	19
Seasonal variations	−1	−2	+1	+2
Seasonally adjusted price	11	13	15	17

(b) The seasonally adjusted price shows a trend of prices increasing by £2 per quarter. To ascertain the forecast price it is necessary to adjust the seasonally adjusted forecast by incorporating the seasonally adjusted price variations:

	Quarter 1	Quarter 2	Quarter 3	Quarter 4
	£	£	£	£
Seasonally adjusted forecast	19	21	23	25
Seasonal variations	−1	−2	+1	+2
Forecast price	18	19	24	27

Task 2

Material price variances = (Standard price − Actual price) Actual quantity
= (Actual quantity × standard price) − Actual cost
= (26,500 × £23) − £662,500
= £609,500 − £662,500
= £53,000A

Material usage variance = (Standard quantity − Actual quantity) Standard price
= (9,000 × 3 kg = 27,000 kg − 26,500) £23
= £11,500F

Labour rate = (Standard price − Actual price) Actual hours
= (Actual hours × Standard price) − Actual cost
= (18,400 × £20) − £349,600
= £18,400F

Labour efficiency = (Standard hours − Actual hours) Standard price
= (9,000 × 2 = 18,000 − 18,400) £20
= £8,000A

Reconciliation Statement:

	£	£
Standard cost of actual production (9,000 units × £229)		2,061,000
Material variances:		
Price	53,000A	
Usage	11,500F	41,500A
Labour variances:		
Rate	18,400F	
Efficiency	8,000A	10,400F
Fixed overhead variances		
Expenditure	300,000A	
Capacity	96,000A	
Efficiency	24,000A	420,000A
Actual cost (£662,500 + £349,600 + £1,500,000)		2,512,100

Task 3
(a) Variances attempt to measure the cost of deviations from planned results. Significant variances should be investigated and remedial action taken where inefficiencies are identified. Alternatively, the investigation may signal the need for replanning if there has been a permanent change in the production process or environment. For a more detailed answer see the section on comparing actual and planned outcomes and responding to divergences from plan in Chapter 1.

(b) Variances can arise because of changes in prices of inputs, changes in quantities of inputs and actual production or sales volume deviating from budgeted volume.

(c) (i) Variances arising from measurement errors where the recorded amounts for actual costs or actual usage differ from the actual amounts. For example, labour hours for a particular operation might be incorrectly added up.

 (ii) Variances arising from out of date standards. For example, where frequent changes in prices of inputs occur there is a danger that prices may be out of date.

 (iii) Variances arising from random or uncontrollable factors. These occur when a particular process is performed by the same worker under the same conditions, yet performance varies. When no known cause is present to account for this variability, it is said to be due to random or uncontrollable factors. A standard is determined from a series of observations. It is most unlikely that repeated observations of this operation will yield the same result, even if the operation consists of the same worker completing the same task under identical conditions. The approach is to choose a representation reading from these observations to determine a standard. Frequently the representative reading that is chosen is the average. One summary reading is chosen to represent the standard when in reality a range of outcomes is possible when the process is *under control*. Any observation that differs from the chosen standard when the process is under control can be described as a random uncontrollable variation around the standard.

(d) The standard price is £23 but the forecast price was £27. The actual price paid was £25 (£662,500/26,500). However, if the £27 represents the current market price the actual price is less than the current market price and the purchasing department has bought efficiently. The reported adverse variance reflects the fact that the standard has not been updated to reflect market changes.

Answer to question 15.18

Task 1

(a) Material price variance = (Standard price − Actual price) × Actual quantity
$$= (\text{Standard price} \times \text{Actual quantity}) - \text{Actual cost}$$
$$= (78,000 \times £20) - £1,599,000$$
$$= £1,560,000 - £1,599,000$$
$$= £39,000A$$

Material usage
variance = (Standard quantity − Actual quantity) × Standard price
$$= (9,500 \times 8 = 76,000 \text{ litres} - 78,000 \text{ litres}) \times £20$$
$$= £40,000 \text{ Adverse}$$

Wage rate variance = (Standard price − Actual price) × Actual hours
$$= (\text{Standard price} \times \text{Actual hours}) - \text{Actual cost}$$
$$= (£6 \times 39,000 = £234,000) - £249,600$$
$$= £15,600A$$

Labour efficiency variance = (Standard hours − Actual hours) × Standard rate

= (9,500 × 4 = 38,000 − 39,000) × £6
= £6,000A

(b)

	£	£
Standard cost of production (9,500 × £184)		1,748,000
Add adverse variances: Material price	39,000	
Material usage	40,000	
Wage rate	15,600	
Labour efficiency	6,000	100,600
Actual cost		1,848,600

Task 2

(a) Material used in standard quantities

(1,500 × 100/80 × 8 litres)	=	15,000
Standard usage for special order (1,500 × 8)	=	12,000
Material usage variance arising from special order		
(3,000 kg × £20)	=	£60,000A
Material price variance arising from special order		
(15,000 kg × (£22 − £20))	=	£30,000A
Wage rate variance arising from special order		
(1,500 × 4 hrs × £6 × 50%)	=	£18,000A

(b)

Revised standard price (247.2/240 × £20)	£20.60
Increase over original standard	£0.60
Material used excluding special order (78,000 − 15,000)	63,000 litres
Price variance arising from price increase (63,000 × £0.60)	£37,800A

(c)

	£	£
Standard cost of production		1,748,000
Add non-controllable variances		
Special order material usage variance	60,000A	
Special order material price variance	30,000A	
Special order wage rate variance	18,000A	
Material price variance due to increase in market price	37,800A	145,800A
Add controllable variances:		
Material price (£39,000 − £30,000 − £37,800)	28,800F	
Material usage (£40,000 − £60,000)	20,000F	
Wage rate (£15,600 − £18,000)	2,400F	
Labour efficiency	6,000A	45,200F
Actual cost		1,848,600

(d) The answer should draw attention to the fact that the divisional total variance was £100,600 but £145,800 was not controllable by the manager. This consisted of £37,800 arising from an increase in market prices and £108,000 arising from the special order. The manager should be congratulated on the favourable controllable variances.

   If the index of material prices was applicable to the type of materials used by the division then the standard should be altered to reflect the price change. The profitability of the special order should be recalculated after taking into account the extra cost arising from the adverse variances and the sales director informed. The sales director should also be requested to provide details of special orders to the relevant managers so that steps can be taken to ensure that the materials can be obtained from the normal supplier.

Answer to question 15.20

(a) (i) An increase in output of 4,000 tonnes results in total overhead costs increasing by £36,000. It is assumed that fixed costs will remain unchanged within this level of activity. Therefore the variable overhead rate per unit of output will be £9 (36,000/4,000 tonnes).

(ii) At 3,000 tonnes budgeted output the costs are as follows:

	£
Total budgeted overhead	72,000
Variable element (3,000 × £9)	27,000
Fixed element (balance)	45,000

(iii) £45,000/(£18 − £9) = 5,000 units

(iv) (5,500 tonnes × £9 for variable overheads) + £45,000 fixed overheads = £94,500

(v) 5,500 units × £18 = £99,000

(vi) No information is given in the question about hours of input. It is therefore assumed that variable overheads vary with output. Most textbooks assume that variable overheads vary with direct labour or machine hours of input.

Variable overhead expenditure variance		£
Budget flexed on output (5,500 units × £9)	=	49,500
Actual variable overheads incurred	=	52,000
Variance		2,500A

(vii) Fixed overhead expenditure variance:
(Budgeted fixed overheads − Actual fixed overheads)
(£45,000 − £53,750) = £8,750A

(viii) Fixed overhead volume variance:
(Actual production − Budgeted production) × Fixed overhead rate
(5,500 tonnes − 5,000 tonnes) × £9 = £4,500F

(b) See the section on flexible budgeting in Chapter 14 for an explanation of why it is advantageous to use flexible budgets for the control of production overhead expenses.

(c) (i) Power for the operation of machinery.
(ii) Indirect materials.

(d) See the section on types of cost standards in Chapter 15 for the answer to this question.

Answer to question 15.21

(a) *Workings:*
Budgeted output = 9,600 normal capacity/2hrs = 4,800 units

Budgeted fixed overhead rate per unit of output = £120,000/4,800 units = £25
Budgeted fixed overhead rate per standard hour = £25/2hrs = £12.50

   (i) *Variable overhead expenditure variance:*
       (Actual hours × variable overhead rate) − Actual cost
       (9,300 × £3) = £27,900 − £28,900 = £1,000A
  (ii) *Variable production overhead efficiency variance:*
       (Standard hrs − Actual hrs) × Variable overhead rate
       (5,000 × 2 hrs = 10,000 − 9300) × £3 = £2,100F
 (iii) *Fixed production overhead expenditure variance:*
       Budgeted cost − Actual cost
       £120,000 − £118,000 = £2,000F
 (iv) *Fixed production overhead volume variance:*
       (Actual production − Budgeted production) × Standard rate
       (5,000 units − 4,800 units) × £25 = £5,000F
       Alternatively, output can be measured in standard hours:
       (10,000 Standard hrs − 9,600 Budgeted hrs) × £12.50 = £5,000F

(b) The volume variance can be subdivided into a volume efficiency variance and a volume capacity variance:

Volume efficiency variance:
(Standard hours − Actual hours) × Fixed overhead rate
(10,000 − 9,300) × £12.50 = £8,750F

Volume capacity variance:
(Actual hours − Budgeted hours) × Fixed overhead rate
(9,300 − 9,600) × £12.50 = £3,750A

For an explanation of the meaning of the above variances see the section on volume efficiency and capacity variances in Chapter 15.

Answer to question 15.23

(a) Because some variable overheads vary with machine hours and other variable overheads vary with direct labour hours separate variable overhead efficiency and expenditure variances should be computed for machine-related and labour-related variable overheads.

Variable overhead efficiency variance:
   (Standard hours − Actual hours) × Standard rate
Machine related = (5,450 × 4 hours = 21,800 − 22,000) × £8 = £1,600A
Labour related = (5,450 × 2 hours = 10,900 − 10,800) × £4 = £400F

Variable overhead expenditure variance:
   (Actual hours × Standard rate) − Actual variable overheads incurred
Machine related = 22,000 × £8 = £176,000 − £176,000 = Nil
Labour related = 10,800 × £4 = £43,200 − £42,000 = £1,200F

Fixed overhead expenditure variance
                    = Budgeted cost − Actual cost
                    = 5,500 units × £20 = £110,000 − £109,000
                    = £1,000F

$$\text{Fixed overhead volume} = (\text{Actual production} - \text{Budgeted production}) \times$$
$$\text{Standard rate}$$
$$= (5,450 - 5,500) \times £20 = £1,000\text{A}$$

(b) The variable overhead machine-related efficiency variance arises because machine hours exceeded target (standard) hours that should have been used for the actual output. Because it is assumed that some variable overheads vary with machine hours the excess usage has resulted in additional spending on variable overheads. Failure to maintain machinery may have resulted in the use of hours in excess of standard.

The variable overhead labour-related variance arises because actual direct labour hours were less than the hours that should have been used for the actual output. This has resulted in reduced expenditure on those variable overheads that vary with direct labour hours. An improvement in the efficiency of direct labour has resulted in the favourable variance.

The variable overhead labour-related expenditure variance arises because actual spending was less than budgeted spending flexed to the actual level of activity. Prices paid for variable overhead items (e.g. indirect materials) may have been lower than the figures used to derive the budgeted expenditure. For a more detailed answer see the section on variable overhead expenditure variance in Chapter 15.

(c) See an illustration of ABC and traditional product costing systems in Chapter 11 for the answer to this question. In particular, the answer should demonstrate how the use of multiple cost drivers should result in the reporting of more accurate product costs than when a single cost driver is used. In order to understand and manage costs more effectively there is a need to measure overhead resource consumption using cost drivers that are the causes of overhead expenditure. Different cost drivers, rather than a single cost driver, provide a better explanation of cost behaviour. Thus multiple cost drivers should also result in better cost management (see the section on activity-cost management in Chapter 11 for a more detailed explanation of this point).

Answer to question 15.24

(a) *Calculation of standard unit cost:* £

Materials (336,000 kg/240,000 units = 1.40 kg at £4.10 per kg) 5.74

Direct labour (216,000 hrs/240,000 units = 0.9 hrs at £4.50 per hour) 4.05

Variable overhead (0.9 hrs at £475,200/216,000 hrs = £2.20 per hour) 1.98

Fixed overhead (£1,521,600/240,000 units) 6.34

18.11

Variance calculations:

Material price: (Standard price − Actual price) × Actual quantity
(£4.10 − £1,245,980/313,060 kg) 313,060 kg £37,566F

Material usage: (Standard quantity − Actual quantity) × Standard price
(220,000 units × 1.40 kg = 308,000 kg − 313,606 kg)
× £4.10 £20,746A

Wage rate: (Standard rate − Actual rate) × Actual hours
(£4.50 − £886,886/194,920 hrs)194,920 hrs   £9,746A

Labour efficiency: (Standard hours − Actual hours) × Standard rate
(220,000 units × 0.9 hrs)
= 198,000 hours − 194,920hrs × £4.50   £13,860F

Variable overhead efficiency: (Standard hours − Actual hours)
× Standard rate
(198,000 − 194,920) × £2.20   £6,776F

Variable overhead expenditure: (Actual hours × Standard rate) −
Actual cost
(194,920 × £2.20 = £428,824) −
£433 700   £4,876A

Fixed overhead expenditure: (Budgeted cost − Actual cost)
(£1,521,600 − £1,501,240)   £20,360F

Fixed overhead volume: (Actual output − Budget output) ×
Standard rate
(220,000 − 240,000) × £6.34   £126,800A

Total variances   £831,606A

(b) The favourable labour efficiency variance may be due to:

(i)   Efficient production in less than standard time due to efficiency of the
labour force.
(ii) Easily attainable standard.
(iii) Lack of production delays.

The variable overheads are absorbed on the basis of direct labour hours and
therefore the variable overhead efficiency variance will be a direct result of
the labour efficiency variance.

The fixed overhead volume variance is due to actual production being less
than budgeted production. This may be due to reduced sales or reduction in
stock levels. However, because the fixed overhead is a sunk cost changes in
volume will not result in a change in fixed overheads incurred and the
variance is of a dubious value for cost control purposes.

Answer to question 15.26

(a) *Standard cost of output produced (18,000 units):*

	£
Direct materials	864,000
Direct labour	630,000
Variable production overhead	180,000
Fixed production overhead	900,000
	2,574,000

(b)

	Standard cost of output	Variances	Actual cost
	£	£	£
Direct materials	864,000		
Price variance^a		76,000 (F)	
Usage variance^b		48,000 (A)	
Actual cost			836,000
Direct labour	630,000		
Rate variance^c		16,800 (A)	
Efficiency variance^d		42,000 (F)	
Actual cost			604,800
Variable production overhead	180,000		
Expenditure variance^e		4,000 (A)	
Efficiency variance^f		12,000 (F)	
Actual cost			172,000
Fixed production overhead	900,000		
Expenditure variance^g		30,000 (A)	
Volume variance^h		100,000 (A)	
Actual cost			1,030,000
	2,574,000	68,800 (A)	2,642,800

Notes:

^{a} (Standard price − Actual price) × Actual quantity
(£12 − £836,000/76,000) × 76,000 = £76 000 (F)

^{b} (Standard quantity − Actual quantity) × Standard price
(18,000 × 4 kg = 72,000 − 76,000) × £12 = £48 000 (A)

^{c} (Standard rate − Actual rate) × Actual hours
(£7 − £604,800/84,000) × 84,000 = £16,800 (A)

^{d} (Standard hours − Actual hours) × Standard rate
(18,000 × 5 hrs = 90,000 – 84,000) × £7 = £42,000 (F)

^{e} (Actual hours × Standard rate) − Actual cost
(84,000 × £2 = £168,000 − £172,000 = £4,000 (A)

^{f} (Standard hours − Actual hours) × Standard rate
(18,000 × 5 hrs = 90,000 − 84,000) × £2 = £12,000 (F)

^{g} Budgeted fixed overheads − Actual fixed overheads
(20,000 × £50 = £1,000,000 − £1,030,000) = £30,000 (A)

^{h} (Actual output – Budgeted output) × Standard rate
(18,000 − 20,000) × £50 = £100,000 (A)

(c) The statement in (b) can be used to provide a detailed explanation as to why actual cost exceeded standard cost by £68,800 for the output achieved. The statement provides attention-directing information by highlighting those areas that require further investigation. Thus management can concentrate their scarce time on focusing on those areas that are not proceeding according to plan. By investigating variances, management can pinpoint inefficiencies and take steps to avoid them reoccurring. Alternatively, the investigation may indicate that the current standards are inappropriate and need changing to take account of the changed circumstances. This may result in an alteration in the plans or more up-to-date information for decision-making.

Answer to question 15.27

(a) It is assumed that the term 'standard costing profit statement' means budgeted profit statement (i.e. budgeted sales less standard cost of budgeted sales). Alternatively, the term 'standard costing profit statement' can be interpreted as actual sales less standard cost of actual sales. Adopting this interpretation will mean that a sales volume variance will not be reported.

Budgeted profit statement:

	£	£
Sales (16,000 units × £140)		2,240,000
Materials		
007 (16,000 × 6 kg × £12.25)	1,176,000	
XL90 (16,000 × 3 kg × £3.20)	153,600	
Labour		
16,000 × 4.5 hours × £8.40	604,800	
Overheads		
All fixed (given)	86,400	1,882,560
Profit		219,200

Actual profit statement:

	£	£
Sales (15,400 units × £138.25)		2,129,050
Materials		
007	1,256,640	
XL90	132,979	
Labour	612,766	
Overheads	96,840	2,099,225
Profit		29,825

Note that the above statements are prepared on a marginal costing basis.

(b) Material price variance = (Standard price − Actual price) × Actual quantity
= (Actual quantity × Standard price) − Actual cost

Material 007 = (98,560 kg × £12.25) − £1,256,640 = £49,280A

Material XL90 = (42,350 kg × £3.20) − £132,979 = £2,541F

Material usage variance = (Standard quantity − Actual quantity) × Standard price

Material 007 = (15,400 × 6 kg = 92,400 − 98,560) × £12.25 = £75,460

Material XL90 = (15,400 × 3 kg = 46,200 − 42,350) × £3.20 = £12,320F

Wage rate variance = (Standard price − Actual price) × Actual hours
= (£8.40 − £8.65) × £612,766/£8.65 = £17,710A

Labour efficiency variance = (Standard hours − Actual hours) × Standard price
= (15,400 × 4.5 hrs = 69,300 − 70,840[a]) × £8.40 = £12,936A

Fixed overhead expenditure = Budgeted cost − Actual cost
= £86,400 − £96,840 = £10,440A

Sales margin price = (Actual price − Budgeted price) × Actual volume
= (£138.25 − £140) × 15,400 = £26,950A

Sales margin volume = (Actual volume − Budgeted volume) × Standard margin
$$= (15,400 − 16,000) × £19.10^b − £11,460A$$

Notes:
[a] Actual hours = £612,766/£8.65 = 70,840

	£
[b] Budgeted contribution margin = Selling price	140.00
Less Direct materials (6 × £12.25) + (3 × £3.20)	83.10
Direct labour (4.5 × £8.40)	37.80
	19.10

Reconciliation statement:	£
Budgeted profit	219,200
Add favourable variances (£2,541 + £12,320)	14,861
	234,061
Less adverse variances (£49,280 + £75,460 + £17,710 + £12,936)	
(+ £10,440 + £26,950 + £11,460)	204,236
Actual profit	29,825

(c) The purchase of cheap, poor quality materials below standard price will result in a favourable price variance but may be the cause of an adverse material usage and labour efficiency variance. Similarly, the use of unskilled instead of skilled labour will result in a favourable wage rate variance and may be the cause of an adverse material usage variance arising from spoilt work and excessive usage of materials. The use of less skilled labour may also result in an adverse labour efficiency variance if the workers are not as efficient as skilled workers.

Answer to question 15.29

(a) (i) Material price variance = (SP − AP)AQ = (SP × AQ) − (AQ × AP)
$$= (£1.20 × 142,000) − £171,820$$
$$= £1,420A$$

(ii) Material usage variance = (SQ − AQ)SP
$$= (1,790 × 9 = 16,110 − 16,270) × £1.20$$
$$= £192A$$

(iii) Actual price per kg in period 1 = £1.21 (£171,820/142,000 kg)
The actual price per kg for period 2 is not given and must be calculated from the data given in the question.

Standard price = £1.20 × 1.06 = £1.272
(SP × AQ) = £1.272 × 147,400 (AQ) = £187,492.80
Price variance (£1,031.80F) = (SP × AQ) − (AQ × AP)
£1,031.30F = £187,492.80 − (147,400 × AP)
$$AP = \frac{£187,492.80 − £1,031.80}{147,400}$$
= £1.265 per kg
Cost inflation = (£1.265/£1.21 − 1) × 100% = 4.5%

(iv) Actual usage per unit in period 1 = 16,270 kg/1,790 units = 9.0894 kg
Actual usage in period 2 = 0.995 × 9 kg Standard usage = 8.995 kg
Change in usage (9.0894 − 8.995)/9.0894 × 100% = 1.5% improve-
ment.

(b) See the section on types of cost standards in Chapter 15 for the answer to this
question.

Answer to question 15.31

(a) (i) A fixed overhead volume variance only occurs with an absorption costing system. The question indicates that a volume variance has been
reported. Therefore the company must operate an absorption costing
system and report the sales volume variance in terms of profit margins,
rather than contribution margins.

Budgeted profit margin = Budgeted profit (£4,250)/Budgeted volume
(1,500 units)
= £2.83

Adverse sales volume variance in units = £850/£2.83 = 300 units
Therefore actual sales volume was 300 units below budgeted sales
volume
Actual sales volume = 1,200 units (1,500 units − 300 units)

(ii) Standard quantity of material used per units of output:
Budgeted usage (750 kg)/Budgeted production (1,500 units) = 0.5 kg
Standard price = Budgeted material cost (£4,500)/Budgeted usage
(750 kg) = £6
Material usage variance = (Standard quantity − Actual Quantity)
Standard price
£150A = (1,550 × 0.5 kg = 775 kg − AQ) £6
− £150 = 4,650 − 6AQ
6AQ = 4,800
Actual quantity used = 800 kg

(iii) Material price variance = (Standard price − Actual price) × Actual
purchases

£1,000F	= (£6 − Actual price) × 1,000 kg
£1,000F	= £6,000 − 1,000AP
1000AP	= £5,000
AP	= £5 per kg
Actual material cost	= 1,000 kg × £5 = £5,000

(iv) Standard hours per unit of output $= \dfrac{\text{Budgeted hours (1,125)}}{\text{Budgeted output (1,500 units)}}$
= 0.75 hours

Standard wage rate = Budgeted labour cost (£4,500)/Budgeted hours
(1,125)
= £4

Labour efficiency variance = (Standard hours − Actual hours) ×
Standard rate

£150A	= (1,550 × 0.75 = 1,162.5 − Actual hours)
	× £4
− £150	= £4,650 − 4AH
4AH	= £4,800
Actual hours	= 1,200

(v) Total labour variance = Standard cost − Actual cost
  ($200A + $150A) = (1,550 × 0.75 hrs × £4) − Actual cost
  £350A = £4,650 − Actual cost
  Actual cost = £5,000

(vi) Standard variable overhead cost per unit
  $$= \frac{\text{Budgeted variable overheads } (2,250)}{\text{Budgeted output } (1,500 \text{ units})}$$
  = £1.50
  Total variable overhead variance = Standard cost − Actual cost
  (£600A + £75A) = (1,550 × £1.50 = £2,325) − Actual cost
  £675A = £2,325 − Actual cost
  Actual cost = £3,000

(vii) Fixed overhead expenditure variance = Budgeted cost − Actual cost
  £2,500F = £4,500 − Actual cost
  Actual cost = £2,000

(b) See Chapter 15 for an explanation of the causes of the direct material usage, direct labour rate and sales volume variances

Answer to question 15.33

(a) Wage rate variance = (SP − AP)AH = (SP × AH) − (AP × AH)
  = (£5 × 53 workers × 13 weeks × 40 hrs) − £138,500
  = £700A
  Labour efficiency = (SH − AH)SP
  SH (Standard hours) = (35,000 × 0.4 hrs) + (25,000 × 0.56 hrs)
  = 28,000
  AH (Actual hours) = 53 workers × 13 weeks × 40 hrs = 27,560
  Variance = (28,000 − 27,560) × £5 = £2,200A

(b) Material price variance = (SP − AP)AQ
  = (AQ × SP) − (AQ × AP)
  £430F (given) = 47,000 SP − £85,110
  $$\text{SP (Standard price)} = \frac{£430 + 85,110}{47,000}$$
  = £1.82

  Material usage variance = (SQ − AQ)SP
  = (SQ × SP) − (AQ × SP)
  £320.32A (given) = £1.82 SQ − (33,426 × £1.82)
  −£320.32A = £1.82 SQ − £60,835.32
  £1.82 SQ = £60,515
  SQ = £60,515/£1.82 = 33,250
  Note that SQ = Actual production (35,000 units) × Standard usage
  Therefore 35,000 × Standard usage = 33,250
  Standard usage = 33,250/35,000
  = 0.95 kg per unit of component X

(c) For the answer to this question you should refer to the detailed illustration of the budget process shown in Chapter 13. In particular, the answer should indicate that if sales are the limiting factor the production budget should be linked to the sales budget. Once the production budget has been established for the two components, the production quantity of each component multiplied by the standard usage of material A per unit of component output determines the required quantity of material to meet the production requirements. The budgeted purchase quantity of material A consists of the quantity to meet the production usage requirements plus or minus an adjustment to take account of any planned change in the level of raw material stock.

Answer to question 15.35

(a) (i) *Sales margin volume variance (Marginal costing):*
(Actual volume − Budgeted volume) × Standard contribution margin per unit
(9,500 − 10,000) × Standard margin (SM) = £7,500A
500,SM =7,500
Standard margin = £15

(ii) *Sales margin volume variance (Absorption costing):*
(Actual volume − Budgeted volume) × Standard profit margin per unit
(9,500 − 10,000) × Standard margin (SM) = £4,500A
500,SM = £4,500
Standard profit margin per unit = £9

(iii) *Fixed overhead volume variance:*
(Actual production − Budgeted production) × Standard rate
(9,700 − 10,000) × Standard rate = £1,800A
Standard fixed overhead rate per unit = £6
Budgeted fixed overheads = 10,000 units × £6   = £60,000
Fixed overhead expenditure variance   = £2,500F
Actual fixed overheads (£60,000 − £2,500)   = £57,500

(b) Absorption costing unitizes fixed overheads and treats them as product costs whereas marginal costing does not charge fixed overheads to products. Instead, the total amount of fixed overheads is charged as an expense (period cost) for the period. A fixed overhead volume variance only occurs with an absorption costing system. Because marginal costing does not unitize fixed costs product margins are expressed as contribution margins whereas absorption costing expresses margins as profit margins. For a more detailed answer you should refer to the section on standard absorption costing in Chapter 15.

(c) See the section on volume variance in Chapter 15 for the answer to this question.

(d) See an illustration of ABC and traditional product costing systems and the section on activity-based cost management in Chapter 11 for the answer to this question.

Answer to question 15.36

(a) *Workings:*

(i) *Material price variance identified on purchase of material:*
Variance = (SP − AP) × quantity purchased
4 November (£1.04 − £10,530/10,000) × 10,000 = £130A
23 November: (£1.04 − £8,480/8,000) × 8,000   = £160A

Material Z stock account

	£		£
Opening balance		2/11 WIP (2,000 × £1.04)	2,080
(9,000 kg at £1.04)	9,360	7/11 WIP (4,500 × £1.04)	4,680
4/11 Purchases			
(10,000 × £1.04)	10,400	20/11 WIP (4,000 × £1.04)	4,160
23/11 Purchases			
(8,000 × £1.04)	8,320	27/11 WIP (6,000 × £1.04)	6,240
		Closing balance	
		(10,500 × £1.04)	10,920
	28,080		28,080

Creditors account

		£
	4/11 Material 7 stock account	10,400
	4/11 Material price variance account	130
	23/11 Material Z stock account	8,320
	23/11 Material price variance account	160

Material price variance account:

4/11 Creditors' account	130	30/11 Profit and Loss	
23/11 Creditors' account	160	account	290

(ii) *Material price variance identified at time of issue of material:*
Using the weighted average basis, the actual issue prices are calculated as follows:

	£
Opening balance (9,000 × £1.07)	9,630
2 November issue (2,000 × £1.07)	(2,140)
Balance 7,000 at £1.07 (£7,490/7,000)	7,490
4 November purchase (10,000 kg)	10,530
Balance (17,000 kg at £1.06)	18,020
7 November issue (4,500 × £1.06)	(4,770)
20 November issue (4,000 × £1.06)	(4,240)
Balance (8,500 × £1.06)	9,010
23 November purchase (8,000 kg)	8,480
Balance (16,500 kg at £1.06)	17,490
27 November issue (6,000 kg × £1 .06)	6,360

Variance = (SP − AP) × actual issues
2 November: (£1.04 − £1.07) × 2,000 = £60A
7 November: (£1.04 − £1.06) × 4,500 = £90A
20 November: (£1.04 − £1.06) × 4,000 = £80A
27 November: (£1.04 − £1.06) × 6,000 = £120A

Note that the entries in the stock account in (a) (i) are based on the approach described in Chapter 15 whereby the stock account is debited at the standard cost and the variances are extracted at the time of purchase. Where variances are extracted at the time of issue, it is preferable to use an alternative approach when preparing the stock account. With this approach, the stock account is debited at actual cost, and issues are recorded at standard cost and the price variances are recorded within the stock account.

(iii)

Material Z

		kg	£/unit	£		kg	£/unit	£
1/11	Opening balance	9,000	1.07	9,630	2/11 Work-in-process	2,000	1.04	2,080
4/11	Purchases	10,000	1.053	10,530	2/11 Materials price			
23/11	Purchases	8,000	1.06	8,480	variance			60
					7/11 Work-in-process	4,500	1.04	4,680
					7/11 Materials price			
					variance			90
					20/11 Work-in-process	4,000	1.04	4,160
					20/11 Materials price			
					variance			80
					27/11 Work-in-process	6,000	1.04	6,240
					27/11 Materials price			
					variance			120
					30/11 Closing balance	10,500	1.06	11,130
		27,000		28,640		27,000		28,640

Material price variance

		£		£
2/11	Material Z	60	30/11 Profit and loss	350
7/11	Material Z	90		
20/11	Material Z	80		
27/11	Material Z	120		
		350		350

(b) The method by which variances are extracted at the time of purchase is preferred because variances are reported at the earliest opportunity. In addition, the stock recording system is simplified.

(c) *Workings:*
   Equivalent units

	Materials	Labour and overhead
Completed production	9,970	9,970
Add closing WIP	8,000	6,000
	17,970	15,970
Less opening WIP	6,000	3,000
Equivalent production	11,970	12,970

Material usage variance
(Actual usage − Standard usage) × Standard price
[6,000 kg − (11,970 units × 0.5)] × £1.04
£15.60A

Labour efficiency variance
  (Actual hours − Standard hours) × Standard rate
  [1,340 hrs − (12,970 units × 0.1)] × £4.80
  £206.40A

Overhead variance
  Actual cost − Standard cost
  6,680 − (12,970 units × 0.1 × £5.00)
  £195A

Standard cost per unit: product X
Materials	0.5 kg × £1 .04/kg	= £0.52
Direct labour	0.1 hrs × £4.80/hr	= £0.48
Overhead	0.1 hrs × £5.00/hr	= £0.50
		£1.50

Process 1

	£			£
Opening balance:			Finished goods:	
Materials:			9,970 units × £1.50	14,955
6,000 units × £0.52			Closing balance:	
Direct labour and overhead:			Materials:	
3,000 units × £0.98	6,060		8,000 units × £0.52	
Materials:			Direct labour and overhead:	
6,000 kg × £1.04	6,240		6,000 units × £0.98	10,040
Direct labour:			Material usage variance	15.6
1,340 hours × £4.80	6,432		Labour efficiency variance	206.4
Overheads	6,680		Overhead variance	195
	25,412			25,412

Answer to question 15.37

(a) *Variance analysis:*

Material price = (standard price − Actual price) × Actual purchases
X	= (£20 − £20.50) × 9,000
	= £4,500A
Y	= (£6 − £5.50) × 5,000
	= £2,500F

Material usage = (Standard usage − Actual usage) × Standard price
X	= (800 × 10 kg − 7,800 kg) × £20
	= £4,000F
Y	= (800 × 5 litres − 4,300 litres) × £6
	= £1,800A

Wage rate = [Standard rate (£6) − Actual rate (£24,150/4,200)]
        ×Actual hours (4,200)
      = £1,050F

Labour efficiency = [Standard hours (800 × 5 hrs) − Actual hours (4,200)]
           × Standard rate (£6)
          = £1,200A

Fixed overhead expenditure = Budgeted cost (10,800/12 × £50)
$$- \text{ actual cost (£47,000)}$$
$$= \text{£2,000A}$$

Volume efficiency = [Standard hours (800 × 5 hrs) − Actual hours (4,200)]
$$= \times \text{ (£50/5 hours)}$$
$$= \text{£2,000A}$$

Volume capacity[a] = [Actual hours (4,200) − Budgeted hours[b] (4,500)]
$$\times \text{ FOAR (£50/5 hours)}$$
$$= \text{£3,000A}$$

Notes:
[a] Note that the CIMA Terminology (1984) describes the volume variance as being equivalent to the volume capacity variance.
[b] Budgeted hours = monthly budgeted output (10,800/12) × 5 hrs

(b)

Stores control

	£		£
K Ltd: X (AQ × SP)	180,000	WIP: (SQ × SP)	160,000
C Ltd: Y (AQ × SP)	30,000	WIP: (SQ × SP)	24,000
Material usage variance (X)	4,000	Material usage variance (Y)	1,800
		Balance	28,200
	£214,000		£214,000

Wages control account

	£		£
Cash	20,150	Wages owing b/fwd	6,000
PAYE and NI	5,000	Labour efficiency	1,200
Accrued wages	5,000	WIP (SQ × SP)	24,000
Wage rate variance	1,050		
	£31,200		£31,200

WIP control account

	£		£
Stores control: X	160,000	Finished goods control a/c	248,000
Y	24,000		
Wages control	24,000		
Fixed overhead	40,000		
	£248,000		£248,000

Fixed overhead control

	£		£
Expense creditors	33 000	WIP (SQ × SP)	40,000
Depreciation provision	14,000	Expenditure variance	2,000
		Efficiency variance	2,000
		Capacity variance	3,000
	£47,000		£47,000

Finished goods control

	£		£
WIP control	£248,000	Cost of sales	£248,000

Cost of sales

	£		£
Finished goods control	£248,000	Profit and loss (P/L)	£248,000

Material price variance

	£		£
K Ltd: X	4,500	C Ltd: Y	2,500
		P/L	2,000
	£4,500		£4,500

Material usage variance

	£		£
Stores control: Y	1,800	Stores control: X	4,000
P/L	2,200		
	£4,000		£4,000

Labour rate variance

	£		£
P/L	1,050	Wages control	1,050

Labour efficiency variance

	£		£
Wages control	1,200	P/L	1,200

Fixed overhead expenditure variance

	£		£
Overhead control	2,000	P/L	2,000

Fixed overhead efficiency variance

	£		£
Overhead control	2,000	P/L	2,000

Fixed overhead capacity variance

	£		£
Overhead control	£3,000	P/L	£3,000

Sales

	£		£
P/L	320,000	Debtors	320,000

K Limited

			£
		Stores control	180,000
		Price variance account	4,500

C plc

	£		£
Price variance account	2,500	Stores control	30,000

Expense creditors

			£
		Fixed overhead control	33,000

Provision for depreciation

	£		£
		Fixed overhead control	14,000

Profit and loss account:

	£	£	£
Sales			320,000
Cost of sales			248,000
			72,000
Variances	(F)	(A)	
Material price	–	2,000	
usage	2,200	–	
Labour rate	1,050	–	
efficiency	–	1,200	
Overhead expenditure	–	2,000	
efficiency	–	2,000	
volume	–	3,000	
	3,250	10,200	6,950
Gross profit			65,050

(c) The difference of £250 in the accounts is due to the fact that the material price variance has been calculated on purchases (instead of usage) and written off as a period cost. In the question the raw material stocks are recorded at actual cost, and therefore the £250 is included in the stock valuation and will be recorded as an expense next period.

Answer to question 15.40

(a) *Material price variances:*
(Standard price − Actual price) × Quantity purchased
A = (£3.25 − £158,750/50,000) × 50,000 = £3,750F
B = (£4 − £105,000/25,000) × 25,000 = £5,000A

Usage variances:
(Standard quantity − Actual quantity) × Standard price
A = (400 × 10 kg = 4,000 kg − 4,800 kg) × £3.25 = £2,600A
B = (400 × 5 kg = 2,000 kg − 1,800 kg) × £4 = £800F

(b) *Labour rate variances:*
(Standard rate − Actual rate) × Actual hours
Dept 1 = (£4 − £11,800/3,000) × 3,000 = £200F
Dept 2 = (£5 − £13,250/2,400) × 2,400 = £1,250A

Labour efficiency variances:
(Standard hours × Actual hours) × Standard rate
Dept 1 = (400 − 8 hrs = 3,200 − 3,000) × £4 = £800F
Dept 2 = (400 − 5 hrs = 2,000 − 2,400) × £5 = £2,000A

(c) Material A price: purchase of inferior quality materials
Material B price: general increase in market prices
Material A usage: inefficient usage of materials

Material B usage: better training of workers, resulting in less wastage
Dept 1 wage rate: use of a lower grade of labour
  2 wage rate: general increase in wage rates
  1 labour efficiency: introduction of more efficient working practices. resulting in a saving in labour hours
  2 labour efficiency: failure to maintain machinery in proper condition, resulting in additional labour hours to complete the operations

(d) (i) *Production volume ratio:*

$$\frac{\text{Standard hours of actual output}}{\text{Budgeted hours of output}} \times 100$$

Department 1: $\dfrac{400 \times 8 \text{ hrs}}{3,400 \text{ hrs}} \times 100 = 94.12\%$

Department 2: $\dfrac{400 \times 5 \text{ hrs}}{2,600 \text{ hrs}} \times 100 = 76.92\%$

(ii) *Efficiency ratio:*

$$\frac{\text{Standard hours of actual output}}{\text{Actual hours worked}} \times 100$$

Department 1: $\dfrac{400 \times 8 \text{ hrs}}{3,000} \times 100 = 106.67\%$

Department 2: $\dfrac{400 \times 5 \text{ hrs}}{2,400 \text{ hrs}} \times 100 = 83.33\%$

(e) In Chapter 15 it was argued that the material price variance should be extracted at the time of purchase. The only justification for extracting the material price variance at the time of usage is for profit measurement purposes. Where the material price variance is calculated on purchases, the variance is charged as an expense to the periods in which the materials are purchased. On the other hand, when the variance is calculated on issues, the variance is allocated to the periods when the materials are issued. For profit measurement purposes it could be argued that material variances should be recognized as an expense in the period when the materials are used and not in the period when the materials are purchased.

Planning and control of stock levels

Answers to Chapter 16

Question summary

For additional questions relating to the calculation of the EOQ and maximum, minimum and reorder levels see Questions 3.10 and 3.12 in Chapter 3.

16.1 and 16.2
Discussion questions relevant to Chapter 16.

16.3 to 16.7
Calculation of EOQ when the purchase cost is constant per unit.

16.8 and 16.10
Calculation of EOQ when the purchase cost per unit varies with the number of units purchased. Both questions require a schedule of costs for different output levels.

16.10
Make-or-buy decision incorporating ordering and holding costs.

Answer to question 16.2

For a discussion of the rationale behind EOQ models see Chapter 16. In particular the answer should stress that some costs will rise with an increase in the order batch size (e.g. stockholding costs) while others will fall (ordering and stockout costs). The objective is to determine the order level at which total costs are minimized. The operation of the EOQ model depends upon identifying the contributory variables and their relevant costs.

The principles of the EOQ model can be used to determine the delivery service which the company will provide for its finished products. The EOQ model might result in stockouts if the lost profits from the stockout are lower than the costs of maintaining additional stocks. Therefore the model can be used to set optimal stock levels and this has repercussions for the level of delivery service offered to customers on finished goods. Similar principles can be applied for determining the level of repair and follow-up service provided to customers. The principles of the

EOQ model can be combined with probability theory for determining the level of service offered to customers, either in terms of delivering products or maintaining a repair service.

Answer to question 16.4

(a) (i) Continuous stocktaking refers to a situation where a sample of store items are counted regularly on, say, a daily basis. Sufficient items should be checked each day so that during a year all items are checked at least once. The alternative system of stocktaking is a complete physical stockcount where all the stock items are counted at one point in time. Continuous stocktaking is preferable because production is not disrupted and any discrepancies and losses are revealed earlier.

(ii) A perpetual inventory system is a stock recording system whereby the balance is shown for a stock item after each receipt or issue. In a non-computerized system the records are maintained on bin cards or stores ledger cards. A separate record is maintained for each item of materials in stores. Therefore the stock balance for each stores item is available at any point in time.

(iii) For an explanation of ABC inventory analysis see the section on control of stocks through classification in Chapter 16.

(b) For the answer to this question you should refer to Chapter 16 (sections on relevant costs for quantitative models under conditions of certainty and determining the economic order quantity).

(c) Normal control levels are the reorder level, minimum level, and maximum level.

$$\text{Reorder level} = \text{Maximum usage} \times \text{Maximum lead time}$$
$$= 800 \text{ kg} \times 14 \text{ days}$$
$$= 11{,}200 \text{ kg}$$

$$\text{Minimum level} = \text{Reorder level} - \text{Average usage in average lead time}$$
$$= 11{,}200 \text{ kg} - (600 \text{ kg} \times 12 \text{ days})$$
$$= 4{,}000 \text{ kg}$$

$$\text{Maximum level} = \text{Reorder level} + \text{EOQ} - \text{Minimum usage in minimum lead time}$$
$$= 11{,}200 \text{ kg} + 12{,}000 \text{ kg} - (400 \text{ kg} \times 10 \text{ days})$$
$$= 19{,}200 \text{ kg}$$

Answer to question 16.5

(a) See Chapter 16 for a graph and explanation of the economic order quantity.

(b) The order sizes are determined by dividing annual usage by the number of orders placed during the year. The order sizes are as follows:

Number of orders per year	1	2	3	4	5	6
Order size	600	300	200	150	120	100

The schedule of relevant costs for each order size is as follows:

		1	2	3	4	5	6
(i)	Number of orders	1	2	3	4	5	6
(ii)	Order size	600	300	200	150	120	100
(iii)	Average stock $(1/2 \times$ (ii))	300	150	100	75	60	50
(iv)	Average stock value ($2.4 \times$ (iii))	£720	£360	£240	£180	£144	£120
(v)	Average annual holding cost (20% $\times$ (iv))	£144	£72	£48	£36	£28.8	£24
(vi)	Annual ordering cost (£6 $\times$ (i))	£6	£12	£18	£24	£30	£36
	Total relevant annual costs (v) + (vi)	£150	£84	£66	£60	£58.8	£60

The EOQ is 120 units and five orders should be placed each year.

(c) Uncertainties to be taken into account are:
  (i)   lead time;
  (ii) demand during lead time;
  (iii) annual holding cost (difficulty in estimating relevant cost);
  (iv) incremental ordering cost (difficulty in estimating incremental cost).

Answer to question 16.6

(a) (i) $$EOQ = \sqrt{\frac{2DO}{H}}$$

where D = Annual demand
O = Ordering cost per order
H = Holding costs per unit

$$\therefore EOQ = \sqrt{\frac{2 \times 48,000 \times £0.60}{10\% \times £10}}$$

$$= 240$$

(ii) Number of orders required per year:

$$\frac{\text{Annual requirements}}{\text{EOQ}} = \frac{48,000}{240} = 200 \text{ orders per year}$$

(iii) Total cost = Holding costs + Ordering cost

$$= \frac{240 \,(£1)}{2} + \frac{48,000 \,(£0.60)}{240}$$

$$= £240$$

(b) Usage per day = 133.33 (48,000/360 days)
   Number of days usage in closing stock = 3 (400 ÷ 133.33)
   Lead time = 3 days
   Therefore the next order should be placed immediately.

(c) Some of the problems which arise when attempting to apply the EOQ formula include:
   (i) Inventory is not always used at a constant rate, but the constant usage assumption is implicit in the EOQ formula.
   (ii) The EOQ formula requires estimates of (1) annual sales, (2) ordering costs, (3) purchase price per unit, and (4) cost of carrying inventories. These items may be extremely difficult to estimate in practice.

Answer to question 16.9

The cost of placing an order when the component is purchased is not given. It can be obtained from the EOQ formula:

$$Q = \sqrt{\frac{2DO}{H}}, \text{ hence } Q^2 = \frac{2DO}{H}$$

$$HQ^2 = 2DO, \text{ hence } O = \frac{HQ^2}{2D}$$

$$\therefore \text{ Cost of placing an order } (O) = \frac{£0.25\,(2,000)^2}{2(20,000)} = £25$$

Average stock level = Minimum stock level + $\frac{1}{2}$ EOQ
              = 400   + $\frac{1}{2}$ (2,000)
              = 1,400 units

Comparison of annual costs:

			Make £	Buy £
Purchase costs				20,000 (£9) = 180,000
Storage	1,400	(£0.25) =	350	
Ordering costs	10	(£25) =	250	
Direct labour	20,000	(£6) =	120,000	
Direct material	20,000	(£2) =	40,000	
Leasing		=	2,400	
			£163,000	£180,000

It is cheaper to make the component unless the released facilities have some alternative use. If this opportunity cost is greater tan £17,000 per annum then it will be cheaper to buy the component. Note that the direct labour is assumed to be a variable cost. The qualitative factors arising from the direct labour force being made redundant should be considered if the component is not made by the company.

Answer to question 16.10

(a) For a definition of variable, semi-variable and fixed costs see Chapter 2. Examples of each cost are:

<table>
<tr><td>Variable:</td><td>Purchase price of raw materials.
Variable cost of placing an order of £50 per order.
Variable cost of holding stocks at £0.40 per unit per annum.</td></tr>
<tr><td>Semi-variable:</td><td>Ordering costs and stockholding costs are both semi-variable since they consist of a variable and fixed portion.</td></tr>
<tr><td>Fixed:</td><td>The £40 element of placing an order is a fixed cost. These costs will consist of staff involved in placing and handling orders, and their salaries will be unaffected by the number of orders placed.</td></tr>
</table>

(b) Annual usage is 6,000 kg ($12,000 \times 0.4 \times 10/8$). It is assumed that the apportioned order costs and the £0.50 long-term holding costs are not relevant costs in the short term for establishing the economic order quantity. Because purchase costs are not constant per unit it is not possible to use the EOQ formula.

Annual costs:

Order quantity £	Purchase cost of 6,000 kg per annum £	Order costs at £50 £	Holding costs at £0.40 per unit (W1) £	Total costs £
1,000	6,000	300 (6 × £50)	200	6,500
1,500	5,880	200 (4 × £50)	300	6,380
2,000	5,790	150 (3 × £50)	400	6,340
2,500	5,700	120 (2.4 × £50)	500	6,320
3,000	5,640	100 (2 × £50)	600	6,340
3,500	5,640	86 (1.71 × £50)	700	6,426

Working:

W1 Assuming constant usage, the relevant average stock is one half of the order quantity. The safety stock of 250 units will be the same for all order quantities and is not therefore included in the analysis.

The order quantity which minimizes the costs in the short term is 2,500 kg.